Mela

Schipperkes

Everything about Purchase, Care, Nutrition, Grooming, Behavior, and Training

Filled with Full-Color Photographs

Illustrations by Tana Hakanson Monsalve

BARRON'S

Photo Credits

Barbara Augello: page 8 top; Paulette Braun: pages 8 bottom, 17 bottom, 20, 37, 45, 73; Paola Visintini: pages 9, 12, 13, 17 top, 25 top, bottom, 28 top, bottom, 29, 32 top, bottom, 33, 48, 61 top, bottom, 77; Toni Tucker: pages 24, 44, 72; John Ashbey: page 68; Jan Mahood: page 69.

Cover Photos

Toni Tucker: front cover; Paola Visintini: inside front cover, inside back cover; Paulette Braun: back cover.

All inquiries should be addressed to:
Barron's Educational Series, Inc.
250 Wireless Boulevard
Hauppauge, NY 11788

http://www.barronseduc.com

International Standard Book No. 0-7641-0337-7

Library of Congress Catalog Card No. 98-10544

Library of Congress Cataloging-in-Publication Data
Coronetz, Melanie.
    Schipperkes : everything about purchase, care, nutrition, breeding, behavior, and training / Melanie Coronetz ; illustrations by Tana Hakanson Monsalve.
        p.   cm.—(A complete pet owner's manual)
    Includes bibliographical references (p.75) and index.
    ISBN 0–7641-0337-7
    1. Schipperke. I. Monsalve, Tana Hakanson. II. Title. III. Series.
SF429.S36C67   1998
636.72—dc21   98-10544
                                                        CIP

Printed in Hong Kong

9 8 7 6 5 4 3 2

The Author

Melanie Coronetz was born in New York City, but spent her childhood in the suburbs along with a Cocker Spaniel, a Miniature Pinscher, and various cats and assorted reptiles. A graduate of Boston College, she studied at the Sorbonne, received an M.A. in French from Hunter College, then taught for several years. Although dogless during this time, she rode horses for animal companionship and wrote articles for national horse magazines. She earned an M.B.A. in Marketing and enjoyed a career in advertising.

When she bought her first Schipperke, she left the business world and began writing fiction. Her short stories have appeared in *The Rockford Review*, *Short Stuff*, and the *AKC Gazette*, where her story about a Schipperke won a prize in the magazine's 1995 annual fiction contest. She began showing and training her Schip, Mercury, and when he died as the result of a freak accident, she acquired two dogs from his line, Monkey and Argo. She trained Monkey to a CD and is showing Argo, a champion, in breed.

Important Notes

This pet owner's guide tells the reader how to buy and care for a Schipperke. The author and the publisher consider it important to point out that the advice given in the book is meant primarily for normally developed puppies from a good breeder—that is, dogs of excellent physical health and good temperament.

Anyone who adopts a fully grown Schipperke should be aware that the animal has already formed its basic impressions of human beings. The new owner should watch the animal carefully, including its behavior toward humans, and should meet the previous owner. If the dog comes from a shelter, it may be possible to get some information on the dog's background and peculiarities there. There are dogs that, as a result of bad experiences with humans, behave in an unnatural manner or may even bite. Only experienced owners who have re-homed such dogs should consider adopting them.

Caution is further advised in socializing dogs with other dogs or with children and in exercising the dog without a leash.

Even well-behaved and carefully supervised dogs sometimes do damage to someone else's property or cause accidents. It is therefore in the owner's interest to be adequately insured against such eventualities, and we strongly urge every dog owner to purchase a liability policy that covers the dog.

Contents

A Schipperke puppy looks like a little bear.

Preface

When you see a Schipperke for the first time, it's like spotting a movie star in your local restaurant; you remember the exact moment, and though years may pass, you vividly recall the details. I saw my first Schipperke on television almost ten years ago. By chance, I had come across a rebroadcast of the Westminster Kennel Club Show, held each February in New York City. There, trotting at the end of a skinny show lead, was a small, tailless black dog whose shape was unlike that of any dog I'd ever seen. The thick, black coat, compact body, and foxy head formed a unique silhouette. It moved with energy and flair.

The next day, I began researching the breed. My husband and I were looking for a dog, but we had certain requirements. We live in an apartment in a city, so an extremely noisy breed was out of the question. A small dog, one weighing under 20 pounds (9.1 kg), was essential because I planned to take it in a pet carrier, on a bus to obedience classes. We hoped to avoid professional grooming sessions, but didn't want to spend hours untangling a coat ourselves. We sought a lively, active companion, a dog that could jog over a mile with me every morning and still have verve to spare. And finally, we sought a bright, "thinking-dog" personality, even if those thoughts sometimes ran contrary to our own. The answer, for us, was the Schipperke.

If you are considering a Schipperke as an addition to your family, this book will provide all the information you'll need to raise, train, feed, and groom your Schipperke, and to care for its health throughout its life. It will also explain the positive and negative aspects of living with this breed.

Of course, even a detailed book can't take the place of a caring, responsible pet owner. If you decide to acquire a Schipperke, it will be up to you to supply the two human elements you'll never find on the printed page—patience and love.

Acknowledgments

My very special thanks to all the members of the Schipperke Club of America who cheerfully answered my questions, in person at the Specialty, and by long-distance phone. Their knowledge forms the backbone of this book, along with information researched from a wide variety of dog-related books, magazines, and veterinary sources. Special thanks, too, to my friend in Belgium for sending me timely articles on the Schipperke. However, this book owes the most to my two buddies, Monkey and Argo, who provided daily insights into Schipperke behavior, and to my silent muse, Ch. Kebrill's Mercury, the little black devil who hooked me on Schips.

Melanie Coronetz
April 1998

What Kind of Dog Is That?

When you own a Schipperke, this is a question you'll hear almost every time you walk your dog or take it on an excursion. People often mistake Schipperkes for Chow Chow puppies, Pomeranians, even Vietnamese pot-bellied pigs, and, occasionally, baby wolves. Yet Schipperkes are not a rare breed. Of the more than 140 breeds the American Kennel Club recognizes, Schipperkes appear in the top 50 of popularity, ahead of New-foundlands, Keeshonden, and Bull-mastiffs. Registrations of Schipperkes ranked 49th in 1996.

A Bit of History

The beginnings of the Schipperke are lost in the past, perhaps as far back as the late Middle Ages. The little black dogs originated in Flanders and the Duchy of Brabant. According to one Belgian source, when the French ruled this region, they prohibited the common people from owning large dogs. Those who lived in areas where the French army was camped, reluctantly followed the rules and bred smaller dogs to guard their flocks and perform herding chores. Thus, in the town of Leuven (Louvain to the French), farmers bred a shepherd dog known as the Leuvenaar. In appearance, it resembled a slightly taller Schipperke and also was tailless. It is now extinct. The name "Schipperke," or "little shepherd," seems to be a variation on the Flemish word, *scheper*, shepherd. The smaller specimens of the Leuvenaar, the ancestors of the Schipperke, were bred to catch vermin and act as watchdogs. Today, this ancient herding instinct surfaces on occasion—many Schipperkes will nip at a person's heels as if keeping an unruly farm animal in line.

When the Spanish occupied Flanders in the fifteenth century, the French regulations against big dogs were abolished. As farmers once again bred full-sized shepherds, the Schipperke found use as a household guardian and rat catcher. In his chronicles of that time, a monk named Wenceslas mentions a small, black, tailless dog, which, he believed, was the devil in canine form. Undoubtedly, this was a Schipperke, and, to this day, they are affectionately called "little black devils."

Tail Carriage

The natural tail carriage of the Schipperke further supports the tie to a herding past. A photograph in an early French book on dogs by M. Megnin, shows a Schipperke carrying its undocked tail like a Groenendael, ancestor of the black Belgian Sheepdog we know today. However, there are also Schipperkes with undocked tails curling over their backs, similar to a Pug or Spitz, suggesting some cross-breeding in the Schipperke's past.

Sunday Collars

The documented history of the breed begins with the shoemakers of Brussels. In 1690 these guild members held a series of Sunday competitions to show off their dogs. Each dog wore a handsome brass collar, crafted by its owner. It was secured with a cleverly designed, and often elaborate, fastener that wouldn't damage the ruff. These "Sunday collars" were kept polished and spotless. They were a source of pride for the craftsmen, and a stylish adornment for their Schipperkes.

Belgian Background

During this period, people in Brussels called Schipperkes "Spitz" or "Spitzke," a name still heard today; it wasn't until the late nineteenth century that the breed was officially christened Schipperke. A pedigree for the breed was published in 1883, defining it as a Belgian shepherd breed, and five years later, in 1888, the Belgian Schipperkes Club was established. Around this time, Queen Marie-Henriette of Belgium fell in love with the breed, and its popularity soared.

The Schipperke in England

Then the English discovered the little black dogs. Soon the British royal family owned Schipperkes; then, it seemed, everyone in England wanted one. Buyers, with money in hand, rushed to Belgium to buy Schipperkes, taking home almost all the dogs they could find. This led to the Schipperke's near-extinction in its homeland by 1890. Alert to this situation, a handful of fanciers began working toward protecting and perpetuating the breed, developing a list of attributes that later formed the standard from which today's Schipperkes evolved.

The Schipperke Legend

Folklore about the Schipperke centers on its tail. One myth states that the shoemakers were responsible for creating the tailless dog. It seems that a shoemaker, angry that another guild member's dog was trespassing on his property and perhaps chewing shoes while visiting, chopped off the dog's tail. When the other shoemakers saw the tailless beast, they thought it looked better, and this started the custom of tail docking. A variation of this story describes a shoemaker who lost one of the Sunday competitions and, for spite, cut off the tail of the winning dog.

Others claim that boatmen, traveling Belgian waterways, were the first to remove the dog's tail in order to keep the Schipperke from knocking over items on board. This brings up the question of the Schipperke as "the barge dog." Though it's probable that some Schipperkes appeared on canal boats or barges, for the most part they were not marine watchdogs.

During the English phase of popularity, prices for Schipperkes were high. Belgians, by nature a practical people, found small mixed breeds less expensive and equally loud in barking.

The "barge dog" theory apparently started with the English, at the time of the great Schipperke buying sprees. Unsure of the little dogs' origins, and wanting to provide a proper history,

Although the Schipperke resembles the Belgian Sheepdog, its probable ancestor, the Leuvenaar, is extinct.

People sometimes mistake Schipperkes for Chow Chow puppies or baby wolves.

What kind of dog is that?

they relied upon language, remarking that the word *schipperke* had its roots in the Flemish word *schip*, or boat, and therefore meant "little boatman." Later, in the United States, this became "little captain," but it is more likely the boat dogs were the Dutch breed, Keeshond, and that they were traveling on Dutch barges. Since the Flemish language contains Dutch dialects, the confusion is understandable.

Schipperkes in the United States

The first Schipperkes may have arrived here during colonial times. Belgian immigrants who settled areas of New Jersey, along with the Dutch, probably brought their little household guardians with them to the New World, but there is no hard evidence to confirm this. However, a Schipperke-like dog, with a tail curling over its back, appears in a nineteenth-century engraving by A. H. Ritchie, from an eighteenth-century drawing by B. Rushbrooke. The dog's companion is the Revolutionary War general Charles Lee, who was captured in New Jersey by the British. Though the drawing is a caricature, making both the general and the dog appear spindly and out of proportion, the distinctive ruff of the Schipperke is evident, along with its foxlike face and erect, pointy ears.

To find documented proof of Schipperkes in America, we must jump ahead to the late 1800s. In 1889 Walter Comstock of Providence, Rhode Island, had two Schipperkes shipped by freighter to the United States. Although he is credited with importing the first Schipperkes, aside from those that may have come with the early Belgian immigrants, he did not turn out to be "the Father of Schipperkes in America." He showed the dogs several times but his breeding efforts were not successful; according to reports of that time, his foundation bitch kept running away, and he finally gave up trying to breed her.

Through the turn of the century, other fanciers bred Schipperkes, and in 1904 the first Schipperke was registered in the American Kennel Club Stud Book. Twenty-nine years later, the Schipperke Club of America was formed.

During the 1920s Schipperke breeding took an important turn when F. Isabel Ormiston founded her Kelso Kennels in Bernardsville, New Jersey. She imported the best-quality Schipperkes from Belgium and eventually established the Belgian standard, the all-black dog, not the English type, which allowed colors such as cream, blond, and brown, as the ideal. Her influence on the breed and her devotion to it makes her the true "mother of Schipperkes in America."

Schipperkes in Canada and Abroad

At the beginning of the twentieth century, Schipperkes in Canada came mostly from English stock. In time, breeders began to introduce bloodlines from the United States, which, of course, was geographically much closer than England, thus making it more convenient and accessible. After World War II the English influence faded and more of the American type, which went back to the Belgian standard, appeared in Canada. Today, many Schipperke fanciers show their dogs in Canada and the United States. Schipperkes with the title Am./Can. Ch. (American/Canadian Champion) have "finished" or become champions in both countries. (see the chapter, beginning on page 66, Organized Fun and Competition for an explanation of how a dog becomes a champion).

English and South African Schipperkes come in colors besides black.

Schipperkes appear in many countries throughout the world, including, Belgium, England, Finland, France, Holland, New Zealand, and South Africa. Though their numbers are small compared to more popular breeds, they continue to turn heads wherever they go and evoke the inevitable question, in a variety of languages: "What kind of dog is that?"

Your First Schipperke

People often fall in love with Schipperkes before knowing much about them as a breed. Their lively expression, glossy black coats, and portable size make them seem the ideal pet, and children think they're cuddly and cute. Yet there's more to the Schipperke than meets the eye. If you are thinking of getting a Schipperke, it's important to determine whether your personality and lifestyle are compatible with this energetic and often headstrong breed.

The Schipperke Personality

By nature, Schipperkes are curious about their surroundings. No matter where your Schipperke is—at home, visiting a friend, or at the veterinarian's—it will inspect the premises. Ears perked, the Schip (pronounced "skip") will trot from chair to chair, looking underneath. Then perhaps it will hop up on the seat to get an overview of the area. But don't expect the Schipperke to settle onto the cushion and relax. In a second, the dog will leap from the chair to continue the investigation. Once the Schipperke is satisfied that all is in order, however, it may sit or lie down for a while, until something, or someone, new to examine appears.

People who like their dogs to sit quietly at their side or settle down on their laps and sleep ought to look for another breed. Those who like to take a stroll with their dog trotting dutifully in *heel* position may not appreciate the Schipperke's inquisitive nature. While the Schipperke can heel properly and walk on a lead, if you teach it, it may

also decide to suddenly about-face and chase that squirrel it spies on a nearby bush. Curiosity and the desire to protect are in the Schipperke's genes, and have been for hundreds of years.

Guarding the Home

Though small in size, the Schipperke behaves like a big dog when it comes to guarding the household and its inhabitants. No strange noise goes unreported, and this means the Schipperke will bark. The mail carrier's footsteps on your front path, the ring of the doorbell, or, for apartment dwellers, the sound of an approaching elevator or voices in the hall will cause the Schipperke to sound the alarm. This is a consideration for people living in apartments where co-op boards or tenants' groups may be intolerant of barking, though, with training, the Schipperke usually will quiet down once the perceived threat has been identified or has gone away.

Schipperkes are suspicious of anyone trespassing in their domain. They will bark, sniff, and circle around the individual, and probably back away when that person tries to pet them. A key word from you, such as "friend" or "It's OK," patiently repeated over time, will help the dog accept newcomers. Eventually, the Schipperke may decide to approach the visitor and allow that person to make friends. And then again, it may not. Schipperkes are independent creatures who don't always act the way we humans want them to.

Of course, a real intruder would think twice before entering a home guarded by a Schipperke. The Schip's bark is loud and sharp, and from behind a closed door, sounds quite fierce. However, though courageous, the dog is too small to seriously injure an attacker.

Playing

Schips love to play. Throw a ball or a soft toy and the Schip may return it to you, though it might not give it up right away or drop it at your feet. In fact, it may challenge you to a tugging contest as part of the game. Or it may decide to take the ball and run—in the opposite direction. Then again, the Schip may roll over onto its back and hold the toy in its front paws and chew on it while looking irresistibly cute. You never know with a Schipperke.

Finding a Schipperke

Though Schipperkes aren't a rare breed, you'll seldom see them advertised in your local paper, or spot their little noses pressed against the window at your neighborhood pet shop. People who raise dogs for profit usually stick to the more popular breeds. How then, do you go about finding one? If you're lucky, you may have a Schipperke or two living in your area, and you can talk to their owners for starters, but chances are you'll have to search on your own. If this is the case, contacting the Schipperke Club of America (SCA) (see Useful Addresses and Literature, page 75) for a list of breeders is the right way to begin. There are, of course, other sources, and this chapter will examine them, as well.

Breeders

You can obtain a breeder list from the SCA by getting the name of the current secretary from the AKC's Customer Service Center, or by checking popular dog magazines for the SCA advertisement offering information on

the breed. Breeder listings will help you find people in your area, or within a reasonable amount of traveling time. This is important because, ideally, you should see the kind of environment your Schipperke comes from. Most Schip breeders treat their Schipperkes like family, giving them access to the house and making sure they're well socialized. It's a good idea to meet the dam and, if possible, the sire. Often, though, the sire provides only stud service, remaining at his home kennel for the bitch in season to arrive from her breeder. By seeing one or both of the pup's parents and interacting with them—after you've passed their inspection, of course—you can get an idea of what your pup probably will be like as an adult. You may also have the chance to watch the pup play with its littermates, a risky move because Schipperke puppies are so adorable you may want to buy them all.

Before you call a Schipperke breeder, however, make sure you've informed yourself about the breed. Breeders often have outside jobs and

By seeing one or both of your pup's parents, you can get an idea of what your pup probably will be like as an adult.

Schipperkes are curious about their surroundings and rarely sit still.

little spare time, and while they'll welcome your questions, they expect intelligent ones. Don't ask of a U.S. breeder, for example, "Do Schipperkes come in white?"

You should be prepared for the breeder to interview you, to determine whether you have the right environment and home situation for a Schipperke. If you live in a house, most breeders will insist you have a fenced yard because Schipperkes have a high energy level and need room to run, safe from traffic. If you live in a city, the breeder might ask if you live near a park or other area where you can jog or take long walks with your Schipperke *on the leash*. Though a first-time buyer may find these questions annoying, answering them honestly will save problems later on. Too many people buy Schipperkes without really understanding what they're like, then the poor Schipperke gets disposed of like an old appliance. A breeder who asks you questions is

protecting the Schipperkes while making sure you are the right person to enjoy the dog's companionship for its entire lifetime.

Tip: Schipperke litters are small, usually three or four puppies. Be sure to ask the breeder how many are in the litter. If there's only one—a "singleton"—find out how it's been socialized. Often, singletons miss the chance to play and fight with littermates, a key stage in puppy development. This could lead to personality problems such as shyness or, on the other hand, aggressiveness, as the pup matures.

Dog Shows

A dog show gives you the opportunity to see anywhere from a few to perhaps a dozen or more Schipperkes all in one place. It's a chance to educate your eye. Look at the males and compare them to the females. Notice their expressions, the set of their ears, the shape and color of their eyes. See how they move. Naturally, if you're interested in a pet, you won't be seeking such quality, but watching Schipperkes in the show ring will give you a good basis for making your own selection later on.

After the Schipperkes have been shown, you can talk to their handlers. In this breed, the handlers are usually the owner/breeders and not paid professionals. Introduce yourself and explain your interest in the breed. You may discover that someone has a litter with a pup just waiting to go to a good pet home like yours.

Contact the AKC or your local kennel for dog show schedules.

Newspaper Advertisements

Generally, Schipperke breeders try not to advertise because too often the people who respond to the ads turn out to be unqualified buyers. Through visitors to dog shows and referrals, breeders usually find the right homes for their show prospects as well as their pets, but every now and then an ad for a Schipperke does appear.

Should you follow up? Perhaps. But first you need to understand the wording in the ad. *AKC* means:

1. the breed (in this case, Schipperke) is recognized by that organization for participation in AKC sanctioned events, and

2. the pup can be registered with them, given a number, and receive a certificate of registration.

The use of AKC in an ad has no bearing on the quality or health of the pups for sale. Neither does *registered* or *pedigreed*.

Champion-sired means the stud dog completed his championship, earning the points needed for the title. This often impresses novice buyers, but many dogs become champions, even some with health problems they can pass on. A reputable breeder would not use such a dog for stud, but often, with newspaper ads, you're dealing with people who breed a litter to make a few dollars or who don't know enough about breeding to produce dogs with sound temperament and healthy bodies.

Champion lines tells you there are champions in the pedigree, but if the champions are too far back, they won't have had much influence on the litter advertised.

In summary, if you do answer a newspaper ad, ask a lot of questions before you decide to go see the puppies.

Dog Magazines

There are breeder listings in *Dog Fancy*, *Dog World*, and *The AKC Gazette* among others. You can find these publications at large newsstands or stores that have an area devoted especially to magazines, or you might obtain one of them at your

An excellent watchdog, the Schipperke often is called a big dog in a small body.

13

When you buy from a reputable breeder, you form a relationship for the life of your Schipperke.

public library. In any event, under Schipperkes in the alphabetical listing of breeds, you'll usually find the names of a few breeders. In addition, the SCA publishes a quarterly *Bulletin* in which breeders advertise, often with photographs of their dogs. You can find reference copies at the AKC library in New York City, or contact the SCA and inquire about obtaining an issue (for addresses, see page 75).

Pet Stores

Frequently, when people decide to buy a dog they first think of going to a pet store. Pet stores offer a variety of dog breeds, plus other animals, all in one convenient location. You can get your pet food, supplies, and puppy care manual the same day you purchase your dog. Though pet stores normally don't have Schipperkes in their inventory, they have sources from which they can obtain one for you. However, you won't have the chance to meet the pup's dam and sire, or see where the pup spent its first weeks of life, and you won't see its littermates and watch them play together. Most importantly, you won't have the opportunity to establish a relationship with your pup's breeder, the best person to answer questions about your Schipperke as it grows from puppy to adult.

Animal Shelters

Unfortunately, Schipperkes do show up in shelters, though not in as great numbers as more common breeds or mixes. Sometimes they are runaways who escaped home without identification. Sometimes they've been given up by owners who thought they were getting a fuzzy little lapdog or the canine equivalent of an obedient robot. Sometimes they're the victims of people dying without having made provision for their pets in their wills. And sometimes, they're mixed breeds misidentified as Schipperkes.

It's a great kindness to adopt an animal from a shelter. Should you be lucky enough to find a Schipperke in a shelter, try to find out as much about the animal as you can. How did it end up there? Has the shelter staff observed any problems? Remember: Here again, you won't have the chance to see the Schipperke's parents or know how it was raised, but if you're willing to work to win the dog's loyalty and to correct any behavior problems it might have, this is a path to consider.

Schipperke Rescue

The SCA has a nationwide rescue system divided by region. This is one of the reasons you won't find many Schipperkes in animal shelters. Rescue volunteers work closely with shelters in different parts of the country and are notified immediately when a Schipperke comes in. Rescue then arranges for the Schip to live in a foster home with an experienced Schipperke owner. This person evaluates the dog's temperament and health and makes a recommendation as to what type of home would suit that particular animal. If the Schip is ill or poorly socialized, the experienced person will keep it and try to rehabilitate it so it can eventually go to a good home. When you contact Rescue and express interest in adopting a Schipperke, be prepared, as with the breeders, to answer a lot of questions about your lifestyle, housing arrangements, and past experience with dogs.

Male or Female?

Many people believe male dogs are more aggressive and females more affectionate, but Schipperke breeders tend to disagree. Females can be quite outspoken and males affectionate, or vice versa; it depends on the individual Schipperke.

On a more basic level, a female may come into her first season or heat any time after the age of six months. Male dogs will try to mount her if you take her for a walk or leave her out in your yard. In the house, you'll have to watch for little drops of blood on the floor or carpet, unless you confine her during this time, for about three weeks. Once spayed, the female will no longer have heat cycles.

If you choose a male, it's wise to have him neutered. Schipperkes don't realize how small they are compared to Dobermans, Rottweilers, or pit bulls, so an unneutered male Schip is likely to attack one of these big fellows, especially if the other is also unneutered. Males like to mark trees, bushes, flowerbeds, and just about anything else they encounter while in the yard or walking on lead with you. Of course, you *can* teach a male not to mark everything, but it takes time and persistence. Apart from these biological differences, both male and female Schipperkes make wonderful pets in the right homes. Ultimately, the choice is yours.

Puppy or Adult?

Breeders usually sell their puppies at about 12 weeks, though some will keep pups longer. Often these are breeders who want to keep an eye on a possible show prospect. Schipperke puppies

Although the Schip dam holds pups by the scruff, you should hold your puppy securely with both hands.

bring their own special magic into a household. Sometimes they are so endearing that people forget a puppy *must be trained*. This means housebreaking, walking properly on lead, and following basic commands such as *sit*, *down*, and *come* (see Basic Training for Schipperkes, page 35).

Schipperkes like to learn new things, but they don't always choose to show what they've learned. If you lack the time, patience, and the sense of humor needed to train a Schipperke puppy, you might want to look for an older, already-trained dog.

Breeders often have adults, from one year up, ready to go to proper pet homes. Sometimes these are show prospects that didn't work out: sometimes they're house pets the breeder kept, unable to find a qualified buyer. Discuss with the breeder the personality and behavior problems, if any, of the dog in question. Some dogs adapt more quickly than others to new homes. These dogs form a near-perfect Schipperke package; they're usually housebroken, lead-trained, and know a variety of basic commands. The only thing they're missing is the cuteness of puppyhood.

Tip: If you're planning to own more than one Schipperke, avoid getting two males close in age—they'll fight for dominance. Also, littermates tend to bond to each other, instead of to their human companions, so it's best to wait before adding a second Schip.

Color, Size, and Coat Pattern

One of the reasons people buy purebred dogs is to avoid surprises. Each breed has a standard or a written picture of its ideal, which literally describes how the dog should look from its ears, to its eyes, nose, teeth or bite, coat, color, size, shape, and tail or absence of tail. Of course, such a perfect animal could never exist, but the standard serves as a valuable guide in helping you form an image of how your dog should look. Even if you never plan to show your Schipperke, you still should familiarize yourself with the official standard, which appears in the appendix, so that you'll know what to look for when you go searching for your own Schip.

Color

In the United States, breeders only breed black. This is the color that appears in the standard, that goes back to the original Belgian standard. In the early 1950s there was an attempt to introduce light-colored Schipperkes in the United States, but the idea did not catch on because it conflicted with the Belgian standard. However, in the United Kingdom, you will find cream and brown Schipperkes today and occasionally white and gray, in addition to black. Countries such as New Zealand and South Africa, following the English standard, also breed colored Schipperkes.

Some puppies with thick gray or brown undercoats may look two-toned in their first few months of life, but revert to black when their adult coats come in. Normal black Schipperke coats may turn rusty red when the Schip is ready to undergo a major shedding, or coat blowing, which happens seasonally or with hormonal changes. This is normal. When the new coat grows in, it is black.

Size

Again, the standard can help you get an idea of how big or small your Schipperke should be. There are no mini-Schipperkes or giant Schipperkes. Ten to 12 inches (25.5–30.5 cm) at the withers is the suggested size for females. For males, it is 11 to 13 inches (28–33 cm). Weight will vary according to size, but most adults tip the scales between 12 and 18 pounds (26.5–39.7 kg). Of course,

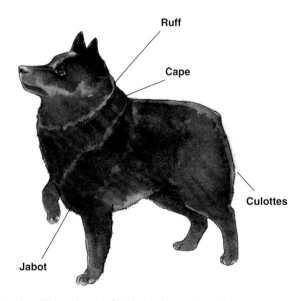

Ruff

Cape

Culottes

Jabot

Though solid in color, the Schipperke's coat has distinct patterns.

these are guidelines and may vary slightly, especially if you've decided to get an older dog or a rescue Schip. Yet, it's important to understand that Schipperkes do not come in small, medium, and large. Though an individual Schipperke may fit into such a designation, a well-informed buyer does not call a breeder and ask for a Schipperke by size.

Coat Pattern

The eye-catching appeal of a Schipperke comes from its lustrous coat, which appears in three distinct patterns. Around the neck is a ruff that leads to another layer called the cape. Across the chest and between the front legs is the jabot. The coat on the Schip's back lies flat, then forms culottes on the rear of the thighs. The standard explains coat pattern in more detail, and describes the correct texture. The coat pattern is in the genes; it is not the result of a groomer's scissors.

Pet Quality or Show Quality?

To novice buyers, the terms pet quality and show quality sometimes cause confusion. What's the difference? Often, it's hard to tell with young puppies. This is where you must trust the breeder. He or she will have had the litter evaluated and decided which pup or pups might work out in the show ring. The breeder is making an educated guess based on years of breeding experience and observing the development of the puppies as they grow, week by week, and play with their littermates. The show dog must conform to the standard and have that look-at-me attitude that will catch a judge's eye. Of course, pet-quality Schipperkes have attitude, too, as well as good looks. But usually they have imperfections, sometimes too slight for the pet buyer to notice without the breeder's input, which could make winning in the show ring an expensive longshot.

Male or female? Ultimately, the choice is yours.

When you visit a breeder, observe how the puppies interact with one another.

17

Price

Naturally, a pet-quality pup will cost less than a show dog, but since prices vary from region to region, and country to country, there is no point in listing them here. Even a shelter or rescue animal will cost you something in the way of a donation. If you've asked around and researched the breed before visiting the breeder, you should have a ballpark idea of what a pup will cost.

Tip: When contacting a breeder for the first time, do not ask the price right away. Most breeders will interpret this to mean that you are too concerned with cost and therefore might skimp on providing quality care for the dog.

Get It in Writing

The breeder should provide you with a bill of sale, a record of when the puppy had its shots, and which, if any shots, are still needed, plus a health guarantee, which attests that the puppy is, at the time of sale, free of disease and parasites. The breeder may also insist you sign a spay/neuter contract or accept a limited registration, which means the pup can't be bred or shown.

This is common practice among reputable Schipperke breeders. Most breeders will also request that you promise to return the dog to them if, for any reason, at any stage of its life, you no longer can keep it.

Buying a Show Dog

If you are seriously interested in a show dog, most Schipperke breeders will insist on co-ownership. This means both you and the breeder own the dog jointly, and both names will appear as owners in the AKC records. You will also have to agree to show the dog or allow the breeder to take the dog out and finish it to championship. This means your dog will travel away from home for many weekends at a time. You will have to discuss and agree upon breeding arrangements, if the breeder wants to mate the dog. Schipperke breeders have contracts covering showing and breeding that you'll be expected to sign. While this may seem complicated, it's an effective way for breeders to screen people truly interested in showing and bettering the breed from those who just want to boast to their neighbors that their dog is show quality.

Bringing Your Schipperke Home

Today, most people realize there's more to bringing home a puppy than carrying it into the house and plunking it down on the floor. If you bought your pup from a breeder, he or she will have explained how to prepare for the pup's arrival and given you a list of what you should buy. Many breeders provide a puppy kit with supplies and tips for caring for your Schipperke. In a few cases this kit even includes a collar, lead, and crate. In any event, advance preparation is a must. Get your supplies first. Buy the food the breeder recommends and food and water dishes. Decide in which room you want to keep the puppy. Then, make sure you've removed anything your puppy is likely to destroy—in other words, Schip-proof your home.

Schip-proofing Your Home

Imagine a little elf, turned loose in your home, with nothing but mischief on its mind, and you've got a Schipperke puppy. Your pup will want to investigate every part of the new environment. Remember, it's in the Schipperke genes. But being a puppy, it will want to taste everything, too—with its teeth. Your puppy doesn't know enough about life in your household to understand, for example, that it shouldn't snack on the fringe of your oriental rug. That's why you need to remove temptation and set boundaries.

The best way to do this is to get a crate, then place it in the area you'll designate as your puppy parlor (see discussion on crates, page 21). The

kitchen works well because it is usually warm and draft-free. It's a main thoroughfare for family activity, which keeps the pup from getting lonely, and it usually has a washable floor, in case of accidents. Or you can set up an exercise pen, a canine version of a child's playpen, to give your pup some running room while keeping it away from people's feet as they move about. Remember, your main concern at this point is to limit the puppy's access to potential hazards so it can't get into trouble or destroy your valuables.

Removing Temptation

Once you've removed the tasty temptations from your puppy's area, inspect the rest of your home for possible dangers. Though your puppy shouldn't wander around the premises until it's housebroken, and then only under your watchful eye, it's possible a family member might let it out by

Tasty Temptations

Chair and table legs (wood)
Decorative pillows (fringe or tassels a plus)
Electrical cords and plugs
Electrical outlets
Floor-length curtains
Leather chairs and sofas
Newspapers, magazines, books
Rugs and carpets
Shoes, sneakers, and socks
Soaps and sponges
Upholstered furniture and cushions

Some Common Everyday Dangers

Inside	Outdoors
Buttons	Aluminum foil
Chocolate	Chicken bones
Children's toys	Foxglove plants
Coins	Lily of the valley
Household cleaning products	Plastic wrap
Needles, pins, paper clips	Rat poison
Thread spools	Mistletoe
Pills	Sharp sticks
Plastic containers	Stagnant water
Styrofoam "peanuts"	Stones, pebbles, seashells

accident, or get distracted by a phone call, and forget the pup is loose, or even step on it by accident. Everyday household items can injure or kill a Schipperke puppy. Objects outside in the yard or in a park, especially during warm weather picnic time, can cause illness or death, if eaten.

Tip: Bring the puppy home at a quiet time, such as a long weekend, when you can spend a few days getting to know one another. Never give a puppy as a holiday or special event present; there's so much activity on these occasions, the pup will get frightened. Instead, you might provide a photo, a collar and leash wrapped in a gift box, or a handwritten announcement of the pup's proposed arrival date. Or order the AKC video on Schipperkes, available from them or through dog supply catalogs.

Prepare in advance for your puppy's arrival.

20

Crates and Beds

Every Schipperke breeder will tell you, "Get a crate." There are several good reasons for this: The crate gives your Schipperke its own little cave, a cozy place to sleep, and an area where it can't get into trouble, and crates are essential during the housebreaking period since dogs, by nature, don't like to mess where they live.

Though some people think it's cruel to confine a puppy or a dog to a crate for long periods of time, the opposite is true. Dogs feel secure inside their crates, and as long as they have water and get their daily exercise, a crate is the best place to leave them—it ensures their safety as well as the safety of your household items. Crates, available through pet supply catalogs, pet stores, or at dog shows, come in two basic types, wire or plastic.

Wire crates. These usually come with removable metal pans that makes them easy to clean, but you'll have to add a cushion, towel, or blanket so the dog doesn't sleep on the hard, cold surface. Some wire crates fold so you can carry them like a suitcase, making them easily transportable, but a wire crate is open on all sides, so you must keep it away from drafts in cold weather. At night, cover it with a towel or blanket to make it cozy. Be sure never to leave your Schipperke in the crate unless the pan is in place as the wire grating can hurt the dog's feet. In fact, Schipperkes that come from puppy mills—commercial operations that produce dogs of all breeds in crowded, unsanitary conditions—probably have spent their days in crates with wire gratings and no pans. Without a pan, the excrement drops through to a receptacle, a consideration when you're mass-producing dogs. Schipperkes with this unfortunate background may have sensitive paws and walk as if they were stepping on hot coals.

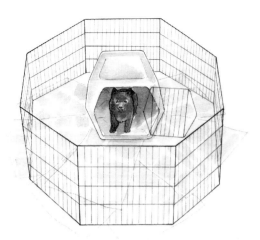

An exercise pen and crate provide your Schip with its own den.

Plastic carriers. These provide more of a cavelike environment, with a solid bottom, a vented top, a handle for carrying, and a wire or plastic front door gate. Plastic crates, which are impact-resistant, provide a safe way to take your Schipperke on car trips. In addition, many airlines approve them for travel. As with the metal crate, you should add a blanket or cushion for your Schipperke's comfort.

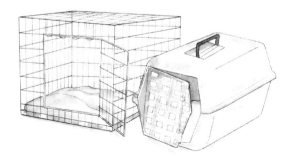

Whether you choose a plastic or wire crate, be sure to place a soft cushion or blanket inside.

How to Select a Crate

Once you decide whether you want a wire or a plastic crate, your next consideration is size. The crate should be large enough for an adult dog to lie down comfortably. This is more important than headroom, since most dogs spend their crate time stretched out for a snooze. A crate that is approximately 20 inches × 27 inches × 19 inches high (51 cm × 68.5 cm × 48 cm) will comfortably house an adult Schipperke. If you've bought a puppy, you should erect a partition to shorten the available space in the crate. This will keep the pup from soiling in a far-away corner.

Beds

If you've bought a crate, there's no need to buy a bed. Often, Schipperkes will sleep anywhere other than on the fancy designer dog bed that cost you a bundle. Many Schips, when not in their crates, enjoy napping on hardwood floors, bathroom tiles, or in the tub itself. My advice? Don't waste your money on a dog bed. Use the crate.

Attention to grooming will keep your Schipperke looking and feeling good.

Tip: Move your puppy's crate into your bedroom at night. Dogs are pack animals, and a puppy, recently separated from its canine pack, needs the reassurance of belonging to a new pack—yours.

Feeding Supplies

Your Schipperke needs its own food dish and water bowl. The best choice is stainless steel. It's easy to clean and keep clean, plus it's chewproof, unlike plastic or rubber, which can cause allergic reactions on the dog's face. Schipperkes eat about a cup (8 oz. or 250 ml) of kibble a day. Though this varies according to the individual dog, you should make sure the food dish can accommodate this amount, with some room to spare to prevent overflowing. If you plan to leave your Schipperke alone for any period of time, it's best to buy a larger water dish, in stainless steel. Remember, your Schipperke must have fresh water at all times (except during housebreaking, which is discussed on page 36). Dishes and bowls come in spillproof models or with their own frames to hold the containers. They usually have rubber tips or bottoms to prevent the dog from pushing them across the floor. Some designs hook inside crates. You can find dog dishes at pet shops, dog shows, or in pet supply mail order catalogs.

Grooming Supplies

Schipperkes require minimal grooming, and that means you won't have to buy a trunkful of supplies. Basically, you'll need:
- a brush
- a comb
- a flea comb
- a few dental care products
- a nail trimmer
- ear cleaner
- shampoo formulated for dogs
- spray bottle
- ball-tipped scissors

The brush. A boar bristle brush or boar and nylon combination does the best job on a Schipperke's coat. All nylon is too harsh and may break the hairs as well as scratch the dog's skin. Natural bristles are firm enough to remove dirt and dead hairs while stimulating the dog's body oils for a shiny, healthy coat.

The comb. A metal comb with widely spaced teeth is used to pull out dead coat when your Schipperke sheds. A good choice is one combining teeth that are spaced wide with teeth that are spaced closer together. The close teeth are useful for combing out a tangled or mud-caked coat. If you cannot find this type of comb, alternatives for pulling out dead hair are the slicker brush or the pin brush.

Flea comb. Choose a fine comb with teeth spaced very close together. The closer the teeth, the easier it is to trap fleas. In addition, this comb can be used to remove fecal matter that often sticks to the hair around the Schipperke's anus.

Canine dental kit. You'll need a toothbrush, toothpaste, and scaler. Be sure to buy a toothpaste formulated especially for dogs; human toothpaste foams, and the dog, unable to spit out as we do, could choke. Choose a brush made for small dogs or use a child's toothbrush. If you plan to scale your dog's teeth yourself, ask your dentist for a used tool, or buy one made for dogs, either the single- or double-headed kind. Canine scalers, made for safe use by the average person, may need sharpening in order to do the job effectively. If you prefer, your veterinarian can scale your dog's teeth but this requires anesthesia, which can be risky, especially with small dogs.

Nail clipper or grinder. People often buy clippers, then hesitate to use them as they fear injuring the dog. The Schipperke's black nails

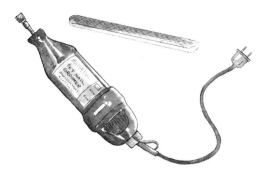

Many Schip owners use a grinder or file to keep nails neat and short.

make it hard to see the quick, or inner blood vessels, which are also dark. That's why many Schipperke owners prefer the grinder. This device sands the nail, removing the risk of cutting into the quick. A grinder, whether cordless or the plug-in model, costs almost ten times more than nail clippers; however, in the long run, it is worth the expense if you plan to do the dog's nails yourself. Otherwise, your veterinarian or local groomer can trim the nails on a regular basis, but you should realize that the cost of these visits quickly can surpass the price of a grinder (see page 29 for a discussion on trimming nails).

Ear cleaner. Use these solutions once a month or more to prevent dirt and wax from accumulating in your Schipperke's ears. More formally known as otic cleaning solutions, they contain salicylic acid plus other compounds such as malic acid, benzoic acid, boric acid, and eucalyptol. They are for cleaning purposes only and are not meant for treating problems such as insect bites or ear mites, which require veterinary attention.

Shampoo. Use a shampoo that is pH-balanced for dogs, avoiding those that promise a silky coat. A Schipperke's coat should feel slightly harsh to the touch and over-conditioning will

If you show your Schipperke in conformation, you will need a special show lead and a fine chain choke.

also should buy one of the waterless, no-rinse shampoos that come in liquid, powder, or foam. These are handy if your Schip suddenly needs a bath after rolling in smelly debris outdoors, or if you want to fluff the coat without having to go through the whole bathing process.

Spray bottle. This is one of the most useful items in Schipperke grooming. Fill it with tap water and keep it in your refrigerator. Spray the dog before brushing to help fluff the coat. Used daily, the cold spray helps promote a fuller coat. In hot weather, carry the bottle with you if you are traveling or out for a long walk, and spray your Schip frequently to help keep the dog cool.

Ball-tipped scissors. A pair of small scissors with ball or safety tips should be part of your grooming kit. They are handy for trimming excess hair from the pads of your Schipperke's feet. The blunted end removes the possibility of injuring the dog if it suddenly wiggles out of your grasp while you're snipping.

Collars and Leads

Collars. A nylon choke is the best collar to use when walking your Schipperke. A 10- or 12-inch (25.5 cm or 30.5 cm) size for puppies or a 14- or 16-inch (35.5 cm or 40.5 cm) for adults provides control and safety. Sometimes called a slip collar, a choke is a flat or braided nylon loop, with a ring at each end. When the lead is correctly attached, and the dog pulls, the collar will tighten or choke, restricting the air supply. When attached correctly, it will release the moment the dog stops pulling. See the chapter on training (page 35) to learn the right way to use a choke collar. Keep in mind that the energetic Schipperke can easily slip out of a buckle collar or an adjustable collar with plastic closures, even if you think it's secure.

spoil the texture. Buy a good-quality shampoo. Since the breed is small and requires few baths, one regular-size bottle will last a long time. You

To properly use a choke collar, make sure it forms an upside down "p" with the tail toward your right when the dog is standing, facing forward, next to your left leg. Attach the snap of the lead to the tail of the "p."

Tips: Avoid chain chokes unless the links are small and close together (fine links). Larger links will break the hair on your Schipperke's ruff.

Never leave a choke collar on your Schipperke. It could get caught on objects inside the house or outdoors, tighten and not release, resulting in strangulation of the dog.

Leads. For a lead, choose a retractable type, made for dogs under 30 pounds (14 kg). This size typically extends 16 feet (5 m), which gives your Schipperke room to run and burn off steam. If you take your Schipperke to obedience school, you will need a 6-foot (2 m) nonretractable lead for the training sessions. If you show your Schipperke in conformation, you will need a show lead with a jeweler's link (fine) chain choke. The most popular leads are made of synthetic leather, which can be balled and scrunched in the hand for comfort while providing a firm grip on the dog. Do not use an all-in-one adjustable collar/lead combination without attaching a choke chain: otherwise, you'll have little control over your Schipperke in the show ring.

Harnesses. Schipperkes with trachea problems often wear harnesses because they put no pressure on the dog's throat, but the dog first must be trained to walk on lead without pulling because a harness doesn't offer the control of a choke. In fact, it gives an untrained Schipperke ample opportunity to pull and get away with it. If you must use a harness, remove it after the walk; it could get caught on an obstacle and panic the dog, and it may also rub away coat.

Toys

Schipperkes enjoy all types of dog toys; in fact, they like to eat them. Therefore, you must supervise play with fake lambskin, latex, rope, and squeaky toys. Hedgehogs quickly lose

Schips are great with children if the child is old enough to understand and follow an adult's instructions.

Schipperkes can adapt to other pets and other Schipperkes if properly introduced.

their spines and their faces if left alone with a Schipperke. Soft toys lose their stuffing. Cotton rope, if eaten, may get caught in the intestines and cause a life-threatening blockage requiring surgery, or pass through the intestines and exit attached to the dog's stool. You then will have to extract it. The only toys to leave with your Schipperke, if you can't watch every minute, are those made of hard nylon. They are safe and practically indestructible. Schipperkes like to chase toys and retrieve them, but it's best to avoid throwing hard rubber toys with uneven shapes. These bounce in unpredictable ways and can hit the Schipperke in the face, causing injury. A good choice for a retrieving ball is a large latex soccer ball made for dogs. It's soft enough for the Schipperke to grab in its mouth, yet it cannot injure the Schip when thrown.

Schips and Children

Schipperkes can make wonderful companions for children, but the child must be old enough to understand and follow your instructions concerning the dog. Before you bring the dog home, explain the house rules to your child:
• If the dog is sleeping, follow the old adage, "Let sleeping dogs lie."
• When the pup is eating, leave it alone.
• Do not overwhelm the pup by constantly picking it up and trying to play with it. Even rambunctious Schipperkes need quiet time.
• Do not feed people food to the puppy or give treats at random.
• Take extra care when opening doors to the outside because Schipperkes are great escape artists and can exit at warp speed. There is a saying among Schip owners: "a loose Schipperke is a lost Schipperke." Sadly, some people have found this true the hard way.

Though there are exceptions to every rule, most breeders agree that if you have a toddler in the house, you should not buy a Schipperke. A child this age moves erratically and shrieks too loudly, which could upset the Schipperke, make it nervous, and possibly cause it to snap. Schipperkes also may nip if teased or poked by a child. This is why the child must be old enough to follow your directions and to understand that a dog is not a toy, but a living, feeling being that requires respect and love.

Tip: Under no circumstances should you allow the Schipperke to play-bite your hands and ankles. This will teach the dog that it's all right to bite people. Schipperkes may be small, but their teeth are sharp.

Schips and Other Pets

Schipperkes have been known to live happily with cats, dogs, and other Schipperkes. A lot depends on the personality of the individual Schipperke and your own common sense. For example, since Schipperkes are ratters, it would not be wise to pair a Schip with a hamster or pet mouse unless you keep them away from one another at all times. If you have a cat, and you bring home a Schipperke, let the cat come to the dog in its own time. They'll probably make friends, or at the very least, learn to coexist. If you already have a dog, introduce the Schipperke to the dog on neutral turf, away from your home and yard. Allow the two to sniff each other and get acquainted. If this takes place outdoors, keep the Schipperke on a leash or it will run off. Once you get home, there may be some initial squabbling over toys and food as the Schipperke examines its new surroundings, but in most cases the animals adapt to each other and form their own pecking order.

Grooming Your Schipperke

Nature gave the Schipperke an outer coat that sheds dirt and a downy undercoat that insulates, protects, and helps repel water. Schips also lack a doggy odor. Elaborate grooming sessions, even baths, are not necessary, but neither is total neglect. Your Schipperke will look best if you establish a simple grooming routine. Once a week is adequate: once a day is better. This gives you the chance to check your Schipperke for anything out of the ordinary, such as burrs in the coat, ticks, or eye irritations. During this daily inspection, it's advisable to check under the nub of the tail for fecal matter. Often, this will adhere to the hairs around the anus, especially if stools are loose. Remove with wipes or a flea comb to ensure the dog's cleanliness and comfort.

Brushing

Stand your Schipperke on a non-skid surface such as a desk or table. Add a rubber mat if necessary or buy a special grooming table from a pet catalog. Let the puppy first sniff the brush, then try a few strokes. Do a little each day until the puppy accepts brushing by standing fairly still.

Brush the coat against the lay of the hair to remove dead hair and dirt. Start at the rear and work toward the front, brushing around the neck and chest. Brush the inside of the thighs, the legs, and the underbelly. Finish by brushing with the lay of the hair, then fluff the ruff with an against-the-lay final brush. Males sometimes leave sticky secretions near the penis that may be removed with a moistened towel or tissue, or, carefully, after moistening, with the flea comb.

Tip: Before brushing, give your Schipperke a finger massage. This stimulates the oils in the skin and enables you to feel any debris in the coat. Also remember never to leave a Schipperke puppy unattended on the grooming table as it may decide to jump off, risking injury.

The handy spray bottle. After brushing to remove dirt and dead hair, spray the dog with water, starting on one side with the hind leg, and working toward the head. Soak the coat through to the undercoat, then wet the other side. Keep a towel handy in case the dog shakes off unexpectedly.

First brush against the lay of the coat to remove dirt and dead hair.

Brushing helps remove dead hair from your Schipperke's coat.

Now dry the dog, rubbing with the towel, then brush as above. If you spray your Schipperke every few days and give a rubdown followed by a vigorous brushing, you may never have to give it a bath.

Clip, grind, or file your Schip's nails to keep them short.

Shedding Time

Breeders call it *blowing coat*, and Schipperkes in this state are said to be *out of coat*. When seasons change or before heat cycles, and usually once a year for spayed females, Schipperkes lose their coats. Over a period that lasts several days or longer, the old coat dies and a new coat gradually comes in, sometimes taking two months or more. Anesthesia, illness, or an infestation of worms also can make the coat fall out, but usually, shedding is part of a natural process. Pet owners should watch for these signs:

1. a reddish cast to the coat;

2. grayish tufts appearing in the coat;

3. large amounts of undercoat on the hairbrush.

These are your signals to take extra care of your Schipperke. Use your wide-toothed comb, pin brush, or slicker to gently remove dead undercoat. This may take a few sessions every day since the coat doesn't all die at once. A bath also will help dislodge dead hair. The hair will come out in clumps, but this is normal. At other times, the Schipperke loses hair in small quantities similar to those left in your bathroom sink after you've brushed your own hair over it. Even Schipperkes that get daily brushing may leave traces of hair on your clothing or upholstery. If this is a problem for you, perhaps you should look for a nonshedding breed.

Generally, at about two months of age, puppies blow coat. The degree of coat loss depends on the genetics of the particular Schipperke. Some lines seem to lose more coat when they blow than others. At about three to five years of age, adult Schipperkes will have a major coat blowing. Daily attention to grooming is important at this time to keep the Schipperke from scratching the dry, dead coat, causing skin abrasions. Schipperkes continue to shed their coats throughout their lives.

Trimming Nails and Pads

Many owners neglect their dog's feet, thinking perhaps that daily romps in the yard or walks on pavement will keep the nails short. Although this may wear down a puppy's nails, as the dog matures and the nails strengthen, routine trimming becomes necessary. The Schipperke needs short nails for comfort and for proper movement. Long nails come in contact with the ground, spread the toes, and can cause sore feet by making the dog walk unnaturally. They can get caught and torn on rocks, rough ground, upholstery, and your clothing. As mentioned earlier, though most books recommend nail clippers, a grinder is easier to use. It trims the nails by sanding, eliminating the risk of cutting into the quick. But it takes a bit of coaxing to get the Schipperke to accept this device.

If you choose nail clippers and do draw blood, don't panic. Take a tissue and apply pressure to the nail. This should stop the bleeding within minutes. If it doesn't, cover with a Band-Aid or touch the nail with a cotton swab dipped in a styptic powder made especially for dogs. You can buy a small vial at a pet supply store or through a dog catalog. The hair between the Schipperke's toes can grow thick, again causing the toes to spread. Trim this with ball-tipped scissors. In winter, in areas where there is snow on the ground, keeping the feet free of hair will prevent ice from balling between the pads.

Eye Care

For the most part, the Schipperke's eyes have few problems. But sometimes, seeds and dirt can lodge in the dog's eyes, especially after it has romped through weeds and tall grass or visited a sandy beach. Often, the normal tearing mechanism in the eye will flush particles to the inside corner

Check your Schip's eyes daily and wipe away residue.

where you can easily wipe them away.

Pawing at the eye, squinting, or a watery eye require thorough checking. In a well-lit area, examine the surface of the eye. It should be clear of any discharge or film. Then, framing the eye with your thumbs, draw down the lower lid. If you see any debris, wipe it away with the corner of a damp tissue or use a canine eyewash solution, applied directly to the eyeball. Inspect the upper eye by pulling upward, while keeping your other thumb on the lower lid. If the sclera or white looks red, this is a sign of irritation that should be examined by a veterinarian.

Note: Dogs have a third eyelid, or haw. In the Schipperke, it is dark brown and appears at the inner corner of the eye, on the eyeball. The haw is a membrane that cleans and lubricates the eye's surface and should not be mistaken for debris or an eye abnormality.

HOW-TO:
Giving Your Pet a Show Dog Shine

It's difficult to thoroughly dry a wet Schipperke, but your hair dryer will help.

For special occasions, it's fun to show-groom your Schipperke. Start with a bath. This removes the oil from the dog's coat, the first step toward achieving that fluffed-up, show dog look.

For puppies, skip the bath and use a spray bottle to lightly wet, then fluff the coat. It's difficult to thoroughly dry a Schipperke because of the thick undercoat, and if left damp, a puppy might catch a chill.

The Bath

Be sure to wear old clothes or a water-repellent apron or smock. Though most Schipperkes settle down and accept their baths—and even enjoy them—it doesn't stop them from trying to shake off when you least expect it.

Bathe the dog in your bathroom or in your laundry room if you have a large sink, and

When giving a bath, thoroughly wet the dog using a hand-held shower attachment.

place a rubber mat under the dog for secure footing.

Use warm water, testing it against your wrist, then gently wet the Schipperke's body, using the hand-held spray attachment. Lather with shampoo, avoiding the ears and eyes. Massage down to the skin, through the undercoat, then use the hand sprayer to thoroughly rinse the dog. Be sure to remove all the soap, especially around the ruff, where the coat is thicker, to prevent flaking and itchiness. Take the water bottle and spray

the Schipperke's face lightly to freshen it and remove surface dirt. Then let the dog shake off the excess water and wrap it in a terry cloth towel.

The Rubdown

Take an old terry cloth towel and briskly massage it over the dog's body, against the lay of the hair to get down into the undercoat. (Terry cloth is better than velour because it is more absorbent and its rough nap stimulates the skin.) Then, gently rub the legs and pick up each foot to blot the pads. To complete the drying process, take out your hair dryer.

Blow-drying

At first, your Schipperke will shy away from this noisy appliance but you can help the dog adjust by letting it see you hold it on your own hair. You may have to do this for several minutes, but eventually, the Schip's natural curiosity will compel it to approach. Then, set the dog on a nonslip surface and run the dryer over its coat, gently and not too close, fluffing with your fingertips. Use a warm setting, and keep fluffing until the coat feels almost dry. Let the Schipperke finish drying naturally in a draft-free place or the crate.

Coat Conditioner and Brushing

The most popular conditioning products are sprays or foams that you work into your pet's coat with your fingertips. The conditioner replenishes oils lost by bathing but won't weigh down or flatten the coat. Next, brush the dog's coat against the lay of the hair, fluffing the ruff and body coat, making sure the jabot, the longer hairs that form a "V" between the front legs, hangs neatly between them, and that the culottes trail in the rear. Feather the hair on the front legs toward the rear legs. Run the brush lightly down the back, from the end of the cape to the rump, to give the correct look as described in the standard.

The Pedicure

Start with the nails, shaping them into neat, rounded nubs. A show dog's nails must be short, making the feet appear tight and compact, like a cat's. Trim the hair between the pads. Most Schips adjust to this quickly, especially if you rub their bellies between snips. The feet, if pressed on an ink pad, should leave a flawless print. The last step is the application of a pad protector cream that helps keep the toes from cracking or drying. Many Schipperke owners who live in areas where the weather is harsh, where salt is spread on sidewalks and streets, or where the Schipperke walks on

Keep the ears clean to prevent wax and dirt build-up.

roads or cement, use pad creams regularly.

Eyes, Ears, and Muzzle

Wipe away any hardened secretions from the inside corners of the eye with a tissue dipped in warm water. Trim eyebrows, the long hairs *above* the eyes, and whiskers if you plan to show your dog with a smooth muzzle. If you regularly check your Schipperke's ears and use an ear-cleaning solution as part of your normal grooming program, there's nothing more to do for a show look. Do not trim the hair in the ears. This provides a natural screen for the ear canal, protecting it from insects or harmful objects.

A Note About Eyebrows and Whiskers

It's perfectly all right to show your Schipperke (or "show groom" your Schip), leaving the whiskers and brows. Some people trim them to give the dog's face a cleaner look, or they've heard that a certain judge—the one at the very next show—

prefers whiskers off. If you are show grooming your Schip for fun, it's best to leave these hairs in place. Remember, a Schipperke can wiggle, twist, or jump out of your grasp in a split second. If you're wielding a pair of scissors near its face, there's a chance you might hurt the dog.

Teeth

Use a tooth scaler or a toothbrush with a small abrasive pad and your special canine toothpaste. Open the dog's mouth and raise the lips to expose the teeth. Gently scrape or brush away from the gums, down from the top teeth, up from the bottom. Go slowly. The abrasive pad can scrape the gums, making them bleed, and a misstep with the scaler can puncture them.

For the final touch, stand your Schip on a table and take a photo or video of your beautiful "show dog." Be sure to reward it for being so patient with a tasty treat—a small biscuit or freeze-dried liver.

Once or twice a month, place a few drops of a canine ear-cleaning solution in your Schip's ears.

Ear Care

The Schipperke's ears are naturally erect, allowing air to circulate freely and preventing moist, bacteria-breeding conditions from developing. Nevertheless, you should inspect the ears weekly. They should smell fresh and look clean. If you notice dirt or heavy wax build-up, wipe it away with a cloth soaked in mineral oil and wrapped around your finger, or use one of the prepared ear-cleaning solutions for dogs. Schipperkes often will flatten their ears and try to wiggle away to avoid having solution dropped in. To prevent this, hold the dog firmly with one arm, then apply the solution with the other. Massage the ear gently to spread the solution.

Normally, Schipperkes' ears are problem-free, but occasionally, they may develop ear mites, which appear as a rank-smelling, reddish brown discharge. The dog will constantly scratch and shake its head. This condition should be checked by a veterinarian. If flies or other insects bite the ears and draw blood, cleanse the bite and apply an antiseptic made for dogs.

Teeth Care

A full set of teeth for a Schipperke totals 42—4 canines, 12 incisors, 16 premolars, and 10 molars. Ideally, they should form a scissors bite, but a

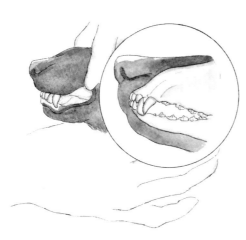

A scissors bite or level bite (inset) helps the Schipperke chew properly.

Weekly brushing and tartar control will help keep your Schipperke's teeth healthy.

level bite is also acceptable for show purposes. A correct bite shows that a Schipperke can perform the function for which it was bred—catch rats and other small vermin. In pet-quality Schipperkes you might see undershot or overshot conditions. Undershot means the lower jaw protrudes beyond the upper, like a bulldog's, and overshot, sometimes called parrot mouth, is the opposite. When the bite is misaligned, the teeth may dig into the gums, causing soreness, or the dog may have difficulty chewing.

Puppies lose their baby teeth at about four to five months. If any of the baby teeth remain when the adult teeth come in, you should check with your veterinarian and have them removed. Retained baby teeth, which look as though they're piggybacked with the adult teeth, can affect the alignment of the adult teeth, causing a bad bite to develop. Once your Schipperke has its adult teeth, it's up to you to keep them in top condition. Frequent brushing, at least twice a week, and removal of tartar is essential, not only to clean the teeth, but to prevent gum disease.

Flea, Tick, and Coat Inspection

Even if you live in a city, your Schipperke can get fleas and ticks; other infested dogs or wildlife in city parks may carry these parasites and pass them on. Though a later chapter (Your Schipperke's Health, page 49) discusses flea and tick control, you should familiarize yourself with the telltale signs of these unwelcome visitors. Constant scratching or biting at the coat probably means your Schip has fleas. To find out, run the flea comb through the coat, paying attention to the inside of the thighs, the area around the anus, the genitals, and the ears. You will most likely capture live fleas or, at the very least, dark grains of grit. Wipe the grit on a

Get your Schipperke used to having its teeth cleaned the first week you bring it home. Go slowly.

damp tissue. If it leaves a reddish deposit, it is flea excrement. You should bathe your Schipperke immediately, then begin the anti-flea procedures found on page 51.

Deer ticks. These carriers of Lyme disease are more difficult to find and are about the size of a pinhead. Once they attach to the dog's skin, they will feel like a grain of sand or dirt, and once they start feeding and become engorged, they will feel and look like a small wart or skin tag. If your Schipperke has not been vaccinated

Three-Step Tick Removal
1. Expose the tick by parting the hair and undercoat.
2. Apply the alcohol with a cotton swab to kill the tick.
3. Grasp the tick close to the dog's skin with tweezers and extract.

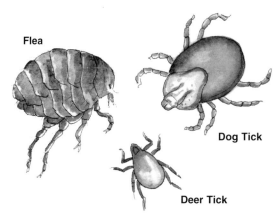

Flea

Dog Tick

Deer Tick

Check your Schipperke for fleas and ticks whenever you've been in an infested area. City parks also can harbor these parasites.

against Lyme disease, you should save the tick between two pieces of transparent tape, and consult your veterinarian.

Larger ticks. Commonly called dog ticks, these can easily be felt by running your fingers through your Schipperke's coat. The female feeds on the dog, then mates with the somewhat smaller male. Before becoming engorged, a dog tick will feel like a scab or a seed covering; once feeding, it will feel and look like a soft gray pea. These ticks also can carry disease and should be removed immediately with tweezers, not with your fingers.

Note: Sometimes the tick's head remains attached to the dog, which may cause a slight reaction or a more serious infection. Consult your veterinarian if you suspect infection.

Baths

The HOW-TO section of this chapter describes the best way to bathe your Schipperke. During shedding, bathing helps remove dead hair and undercoat. Baths also kill fleas, but in general, a spray bottle filled with water or the no-rinse shampoo can take the place of a tub bath.

Basic Training for Schipperkes

Schipperkes are constantly on the move, often at amazing speed. To keep your pet out of trouble, you must channel this energy into good behavior. This means training on a daily basis from the time you get your puppy until it can walk on a lead without pulling and learns the basic commands: *sit*, *stay*, *down*, and *come*. You'll need to devote the first year of your Schipperke's life to basic training. *If your life is too hectic to spend time training the puppy, please do not get a Schipperke.* People who think these are sweet little dogs that will obey at all times are buying the wrong breed, and more often than not, these poor Schipperkes end up in the pound, or are hit by a car. You must train and train properly from the moment your pup comes home.

A good place to start is a puppy kindergarten course, sometimes offered by your local humane society, animal shelter, or an obedience training school. Check your phone book for listings or inquire on the Internet. Before you enroll, you can give your Schip a headstart by training at home with the guidelines in this chapter.

Note: Exercises in this chapter should be done on lead. Be prepared to crouch down to your Schipperke's level so you don't loom like a giant. If you prefer using a table for teaching *sit* and *down*, you'll first need to train your Schipperke to stay still on the table. Depending on the dog, this could delay your overall training program.

Using the Crate

Think of the crate as a baseball dugout. It's your Schipperke's bench when it's not on the playing field, or in this case, being trained. Though Schipperkes prefer being where the action is, they will accept the crate, some more readily than others. Be sure to provide fresh water and a chew toy, such as a hard nylon bone, never rawhide or soft toys.

Every time you put your Schip in the crate, say, "Skippy, go inside" and give a small treat to make this inviting. Eventually, you'll only have to open the door and give the command. If your Schip rolls onto its back and goes limp to avoid being crated, do not drag it or try to lift it. Clap your hands sharply. Startled, it'll jump to its feet. Then place it in the crate, giving praise and a treat. If your Schip constantly whines when crated and doesn't respond to your voice command for silence, surprise it with a sharp noise—either rattle the coin can (see page 42) or kick the crate once, saying, "Quiet now," or "Enough." Once your pup is reliably house-trained, you can leave the crate door open so it may go in and out whenever it wants.

The Traveling Case

This is also a good time to get your Schipperke used to a soft-sided traveling case. Sold under various brand names, these nylon cases are useful for traveling by plane, train, taxi, or bus. Unzip the end of the bag, place a treat inside, and say, "Skippy, go inside." Most Schipperkes, out of curiosity, will want to investigate. Once inside, praise your Schip, but don't close the bag. Do this several times, then close the bag—with praise, of course. Use a trail of treats if your Schip seems hesitant about entering the bag, but remain patient. Do not open the top of the bag and shove the dog in, or it will view this as a negative experience.

Housebreaking

Schipperkes are not the easiest dogs to housebreak, but neither are they the most difficult. Success will depend on how diligently you adhere to a fixed schedule. A two- to three-month-old puppy has a small bladder and bowel capacity, and cannot "hold it" for more than four hours at a time, except when sleeping at night. During the housebreaking period, which may take a solid week or longer, you should confine your Schipperke to the crate except for feeding, playtime, and "going potty" outdoors. Pups need to eliminate upon awakening, about 20 minutes after eating, and before turning in for the night. Since a puppy up to age six months usually eats four times a day, this means a minimum of six potty sessions.

Paper Training

People who work outside the home face a challenge, and many choose paper training as a method of housebreaking. They use newspaper or special pads, scented to encourage the pup to eliminate, and place them in the potty area indoors. They gradually take away the paper, leaving a smaller potty area, then (and by now the pup is older and can wait longer) they remove the paper and take the dog outdoors. Some owners use paper for the entire life of the dog, but risk coming home to a place that has a certain odor.

Odor-Neutralizing Products

Whichever method you choose, be consistent, and be sure to stock up on the special products that neutralize the odor of canine urine and feces. If your pup soils indoors, you must deodorize the spot or it will soil there again. Soap and water will not cover the scent. Dogs have a highly developed sense of smell, and while a human may not detect an odor, the dog will know it's there. Your puppy may occasionally have accidents in the house, even at age six or seven months. If these are frequent, and your veterinarian agrees there is no illness causing them, start the housebreaking program again.

Note: Sometimes paper training backfires and Schips trained to paper may think it's all right to use the Sunday *Bugle* you left lying on the floor in your den. If possible, train your Schipperke to eliminate outdoors.

Housebreaking Hints

1. Sniffing and circling mean take the pup outside.
2. Watch that it "does its business."
3. Place prescented pads outside in the potty area.
4. Praise the pup when it does its business.
5. Say "Go potty" or "Do your business" to aid training.
6. Never rub the pup's face in mistakes.
7. Only reprimand the pup if you catch it in the act of messing.
8. Never use physical punishment. Use your voice, then rush the pup outside or to a newspapered area.
9. Stick to the schedule.
10. Be patient.

Table Manners (Part I)

Schipperkes are expert beggars. They'll do anything to get a taste of the food that's on *your* plate; therefore you must resolve never to feed your Schip from the table. If you do, you'll create a pest that will never take No for an answer. Inform all family members and visitors that even the smallest tidbit should not be given to the pup while you or they are at the table. If the Schip puts paws on your lap while you're seated, gently remove them, saying "Off," then add "I'm busy." You may have to do this dozens of times over a period of weeks or months, but don't lose patience. Your Schipperke understands what you're saying, but it also knows what it wants. Remember, Schips are headstrong. The trick to training them is to reward good behavior by providing opportunities for them to do what you want them to do.

Note: Do not say "Down " when you mean "Get off." "Down" means lie down and is a command used in obedience training. Use "Off" if your Schip jumps on you or whenever you want it to remove itself from a forbidden piece of furniture.

Schips are expert beggars. Never feed your Schipperke from the table.

Table Manners (Part II)

Many Schipperkes, especially young puppies, like to puddle around in their water dishes and play with their food. Nuggets get bounced along the floor or dragged into another area for future snacking. Don't allow this or one day you may find food crunched on the living room rug or attracting ants in your bedroom. If you see your Schip removing food from the dish, say "No," return it to the dish, and tell it, "Eat here." At first it may think this is a new game but when it takes a few bites from the dish and eats correctly, praise it. Be consistent and firm, but not overbearing. Remember to make the correction *while* the dog is misbehaving, not after the fact. Dogs live in the present and will not associate their actions of ten minutes ago with a tardy correction.

Tip: Develop a training vocabulary and use it consistently. Don't just say "No " to undesirable behavior. The dog soon will ignore you if all it hears is "no, no, no, no, no."

Commands

Sit

Many Schipperkes come from their breeders already knowing the *sit* command, but if yours doesn't, it's easy to teach. Place the training leash and collar on your Schipperke, holding your hand near the snap of the leash. Pull up on the collar, and push down, gently but firmly, on the rear while saying, "Skippy, sit." Or, using a treat, trail it from eye level to slightly above the dog's head, then back behind the ears. Tell the dog to sit. As it follows the treat, it'll sit. If it jumps, the treat is too high above the head. Withhold the treat and start again.

For training, use a 6-foot (1.8 m) lead. You'll have better control than with the 16-foot (5 m) retractable lead. Use your nylon choke or a fine link metal choke, releasing quickly after the correction. Never pull or drag your Schipperke or allow this collar to literally choke the dog by holding it tightly on its neck. *Always remove it after the training session.* You may use a buckle collar if you are training in an enclosed area where there is no chance for your Schipperke to slip out of the collar and escape.

Stay

Whenever you want your Schip to remain in a certain position, say, "Stay." In formal obedience training, stay is used with *stand*, *sit*, and *down*. Sit your Schipperke on your left side. Place the palm of your hand in front of

Schips learn "Down" quickly if you use treats.

its face and say, "Skippy, stay." Take a step forward and face your Schip. Guaranteed, the dog will follow you. Return it to the sit position and repeat the command. Most Schips pick this up after a few tries. Once yours has the idea, step farther away each time, until you are at the end of the lead, facing your sitting Schipperke.

Down

Schipperkes learn this very quickly once they've mastered sit. From the sit, hold a treat so the dog can smell it. Draw your hand toward the floor and say, "Skippy, down." Feed the treat as it reaches for it. In just a few tries, most Schipperkes learn this exercise. Another approach is to place your right hand on the leash, near the snap, and rest your left hand on the shoulders while the dog is sitting. Gently push sideways, making it lose its balance, and pull down on the collar. Say, "Skippy, down." Some dogs, especially those with alpha personalities, may resist this technique. Do not force the dog or apply strong pressure. Return to the method with treats. For variety, practice the *stay* command in the *down* position.

Walking on Lead

This sounds simple, but it is one of the hardest feats to accomplish with a Schipperke. Their high energy level and desire to investigate their surroundings will have them tugging on the leash and zigzagging at every opportunity. Even if you plan to let your Schipperke run free in your fenced yard most of the time, you should train it to walk on a lead for visits to the veterinarian and excursions.

Your goal is to have it on a slack lead, walking on your left side, in the direction *you* choose. When your Schipperke matures, at age two or three, you can teach heeling, but for now, strive for control.

Most Schipperkes coming from breeders already are familiar with wearing a collar and leash. If yours isn't, place a *buckle* collar around its neck, and using the training lead, let it trail it around the house or yard while you watch. If it tries to chew it, take it out of its mouth and say, "No chew." In stubborn cases, dab vinegar or bitter apple on the lead, put it in the Schip's mouth and repeat, "No chew. Not for Skippy."

Once the dog accepts the lead, you're ready for the next step, walking together. Your Schipperke will try to dash out the door like a cannonball every time you open it to go outdoors. To counteract this, make it sit. Tell it "Skippy, wait," then "Walk easy." Repeat every time it plunges ahead, even if it takes you ten minutes to get off the front porch. While walking, use a sharp leash correction (a quick snap or jerk, then release) and voice command to get the attention back to walking. Surprise the dog with a quick change of direction or an about-turn— a complete turn in the opposite direction—to break a pattern of pulling or zigzagging across your path. Use treats to keep the dog by your side. Slap your left thigh and say, "By me," or "Here" to show it where you want it, then feed the treat.

Tip: The key to keeping your Schipperke's attention is to keep it interested. You may have to experiment with different techniques (and treats) to find what works best.

Come!

Come, or the recall, is one of the most enjoyable commands to teach a Schipperke; when the Schip gets the idea, it'll launch its body like a rocket and zoom toward you at warp speed. For best results, teach this on a long line (an inexpensive 15-foot (4.6 m) cotton web or nylon lead), so you have control over the dog at all times. Let

Use a long line to teach the recall or "come." *Never let your Schipperke off the leash unless you're fenced in.*

your Schip walk out on the line, and when it's a few feet (meters) away, call it, "Skippy, come." If it hesitates, give a gentle tug on the line, and offer a treat. You may have to draw the lead in the first time. Praise the Schip and reward it with the treat. Do this a few times each day. After a while, train where there are distractions such as bicycle riders and other dogs. In the event your Schip yanks the leash out of your hand and takes off, try very hard to stay calm. Do not run after it, shrieking its name. It'll only run faster—away from you. Call it in a happy voice and tell it "Treat" or "Yum yum" or whatever word you're using for food rewards. Kneel and open your arms in a welcoming pose. When it comes back, be sure you feed the treat or this never will work again. Another technique is to walk away from the dog, saying "Good-bye, Skippy." You might crouch to make yourself "disappear" into the distance. Soon your Schip will come running, thinking you've gone home without it, and home, of course, means food. Don't forget to praise it for coming.

Training Tips
1. Keep sessions short (10 to 15 minutes).
2. Use food rewards (small pieces).
3. Give lots of praise.
4. Avoid physical punishment.
5. Train in a quiet place at first.
6. Say the dog's name, then give the command.
7. Use a cheerful tone of voice.
8. Make training fun.

Note: No matter how well trained, never trust a Schipperke off lead, outdoors, in an unfenced area. You may say "Skippy, come," and it'll think, "Later, Mom, first I need to chase that squirrel across the busy highway."

Don't Come
This is not a real command, but unfortunately many people teach it to their dogs. If the dog doesn't come right away, they'll shout, "You come, bad dog!" And when the poor dog does, they'll grab the collar and scold it. The dog then thinks it's being corrected for coming. Never punish your Schipperke for coming, no matter how long it takes. Always make returning

Say "Off" when you mean "Get off." Do not use "Down."

to you a happy experience. Give a treat and praise, or follow up with a brief period of play.

"Dead Dog"
One of the ways to make training fun is to teach your Schipperke some tricks based on the serious commands it knows. "Dead dog" uses the *down*. The goal is to have the dog lie down, then roll onto its side and play dead. Make your hand into a gun, with the thumb up and the index finger extended. Point to your Schip and give the *down* command. Feed a treat once it's down.

Next, you have to coax it to lie on its side. Hold a treat above its head, off to the side, and tell it "Over." At first, it'll get up and try to snag the treat. Tell it "Down," using your finger gun. Then try "Over" again. This may take a while. Don't guide it all the way over. Let it fall back so it's lying on its side, in the "dead" position. Say "Dead dog" and give a treat. Practice this trick step by step and be patient. Eventually, you'll point your "gun" at the Schip, say "Bang" instead of "Down" and watch your little devil hit the ground to the amusement of your friends, or even your local police officer.

A Few Words about Discipline
Schips generally, prefer their idea of fun (chasing squirrels or poking around new places) to your ideas for training—"Come, Schipperke, let's practice walking quietly on lead." Though they enjoy learning new commands, they soon get bored, testing your patience.

Never yell at your Schipperke, hit or abuse it in any way. A Schip is a small dog and physical punishment can injure it, but more importantly, it can scar it mentally, making it think you don't like it, and turning it into a fearful dog. You must therefore outsmart your Schipperke by diverting its attention from unacceptable behavior, then rewarding and praising it for listening to you.

Your voice, used with proper tone and volume, is a valuable tool. For example, say "Aaack" in a loud, deep voice. This stops the Schip in its tracks. Then immediately tell it what you want: "Drop that" (if it's chomping your slippers), and say "Not for Skippy." Substitute a chew toy and tell it, "This is for Skippy." Then praise it and tell it it's a good dog. This takes work and it takes time, plus a huge amount of patience, but this approach will develop a cheerful, obedient, well-adjusted Schipperke.

Never say your Schipperke's name in an angry voice or let impatience take over when you give a command. Schips learn best when they're having fun.

Behaving at the Veterinarian's

On the Table

The veterinarian will examine your Schipperke on a stainless steel table. To prepare for your first visit, practice at home on formica, marble, glass (though you'd better be sure its nails are short or the dog will leave scratch marks), or smooth wood. Place the Schip's front feet on the front edge of the table or countertop, so if it moves forward, it'll fall (naturally, you'll catch it). Tell it to stand. Praise it if it does.

To prevent the dog from backing away, position the back feet on the rear edge of the surface. Use a surface next to a wall to curb sidestepping. This is also the way to train a show dog to stand on the table so the judge can examine it.

Dental Checkup

Open your Schipperke's mouth. Run your thumb and index fingers over its gums, praising if it doesn't pull away. Tell it "No bite" *if* it nibbles (licking is OK). Conformation Schipperkes have

Handy Training Words

Off = Get off.
I'm busy = Go away, don't bother me now.
Enough! = Quit it!
Not for (pet's name). = This isn't for you, Schipperke.
This is for (pet's name). = This is for you, Schipperke.
Wait = Hold up, don't move another inch.
Stay = Remain where you are (sitting, lying down).
Down = Assume the *down* position.
Here or *By me* = This is where I want you.
Aaack (or similar sound) = Listen, now.
Treat or *Yum Yum* = I have something good for you.

their bites checked by the judge to see if the bites are correctly scissors or level. To get your Schip used to this (even if the only *judge* is your veterinarian), hold it under the chin with one hand, then place the thumb and index finger of your other hand on the upper lips, behind the nose, and lift the lips, exposing the front teeth to reveal the bite.

Teach your Schip to stand quietly on a table for veterinary visits, and perhaps, dog shows.

Handling the Hindquarters

The veterinarian may need to take your Schip's temperature or perform a rectal exam. To acclimate your puppy, give a finger massage, scratching the inner and outer thighs and the entire hind end. Some Schipperkes are fidgety around the nub of their tails and need a very light touch. If you have a male show prospect, you must accustom him to having his testicles touched. Through touch, a dog show judge determines that the male is intact, with both testicles descended, a necessity for exhibiting in the breed ring (see pages 66–69 for more information about showing).

A prong collar can curb aggressive pullers, but you must learn how to use it properly.

Managing a Difficult Schipperke

Some Schipperkes are more headstrong than others, and if you own one that's tough, you might need to use more than your voice when training.

Coin Can

A sudden, sharp noise will get your dog's attention. Put a few coins in an empty can, tape it closed, and shake it loudly near the dog, firmly saying, "No, stop that," or "Enough." The coin can is effective to curtail barking, jumping on people, and unacceptable acts, such as digging in the garden. If you have other pets in the house, however, be aware that the noise will affect them, too.

Prong or Pinch Collar

This is an extreme device that should be used only under the guidance of an experienced trainer. It is a metal choke collar with prongs that pinch the dog's neck when the collar is tightened. It can be used for training a dog that pulls excessively, lunges at other dogs, or refuses to walk by your side; however, sometimes, new pet owners run out and buy one of these collars because a friend says, "Hey, try a pinch collar." Most prong collars are too big for Schipperkes and can cause severe damage. There are specialty training suppliers who offer "mini" or "micro" prong collars for small dogs. If your Schipperke is this hard to train, it's best to find a good obedience school or trainer, and only then consider a micro prong collar.

Feeding Your Schipperke

Whether your Schipperke is a picky eater or a real chow hound, it's important to feed a well-balanced diet in quantities recommended for a Schipperke-sized dog. The right nutrients in the *right proportions* provide the building blocks for strong teeth and bones, proper growth, and overall good health. Fortunately, today's dog food manufacturers recognize this, and most good-quality commercial dog foods provide the dietary essentials your Schipperke needs. But dog food labels can be confusing, with strange-sounding ingredients such as pyridoxine hydrochloride (vitamin B_6) listed among such commonplace foods as chicken and corn. To understand exactly what's in that bag, box, or can, it's important to know what a dog's daily diet should include.

Components of a Healthy Diet

Protein

Dogs need protein for cell growth and repair, for energy, and for overall good health. An average adult dog's diet should include at least 22 percent protein. Pregnant bitches or dogs in competition, with highly active lifestyles or spending lots of time outdoors in the cold, usually require a higher amount. Both grains and meat contain protein but for Schipperkes, meat is a better source. It contains the amino acids arginine and cystine, which are essential for good skin and coat, and a thick, healthy coat is one of the breed's eye-catching features.

Meats used in commercial dog foods generally come from poultry, beef, and lamb. Some specialty brands offer delicacies such as venison and rabbit.

Vegetable proteins usually are derived from glutens, commonly corn gluten, and soybean meal. These are grain "fractions," not whole grains, and therefore are less nutritious. Some manufacturers use these fillers because they are cheaper than meat but for a dog, foods containing vegetable protein fillers aren't as tasty as meat-based products. However, all meat proteins are not equal. The word *meal* is a sign of by-products—a mix of innards, often containing hearts, livers, gizzards, and intestines, which can also be nutritious if offered in a premium brand where quality control is enforced. The easiest and best way to choose the food for your Schipperke is to follow your breeder's recommendation.

Fats and Carbohydrates

Fats play an equally important role in nourishing your Schipperke, both as a concentrated source of energy and as a source of the fatty acids needed for healthy skin and coat. Linoleic acid, one of the Omega 6 fatty acids, helps promote good coat and skin, and it should form part of your Schipperke's diet. Most manufacturers of quality commercial foods recognize this and have incorporated fatty acids into their formulas. In general, foods with higher concentrations of linoleic acid in their fats are more expensive.

Schips need adequate protein and fat for a shiny, healthy coat.

tions. They help stimulate the dog's enzyme systems. Minerals, too, are components of the important chemical reactions that take place in the dog's body, but too much of either could lead to trouble-causing imbalances.

Commercial foods offering *complete nutrition* provide the right amounts of vitamins a healthy Schip will need, including the important B-complex group. The same holds true for minerals. Calcium and phosphorous are essential for strong bones and teeth. About a dozen other minerals, such as manganese, copper, and zinc, appear in smaller doses or trace amounts and complete the balance of nutrients a normal Schip requires.

Canned, Dry, or Semimoist?

Commercial foods come in three distinct forms: canned, dry, and semi-moist. Most Schipperke owners prefer dry food or kibble. As the dog chews, the dry food particles rub against its teeth, which helps reduce tartar build-up and discoloration, often a problem with Schipperkes, depending on their bloodlines or the mineral content of their drinking water. Dry food is convenient and travels well. Though it doesn't require refrigeration, it should be kept away from heat, in a dry place, and be sealed tightly in its bag or container after each use. Dry food may safely be left in the dish if you allow your Schip to nibble at its food over the course of the day, known as free-choice feeding. Many good-quality commercial dry foods come in Schipperke-sized bits, small nuggets, or triangles that are easier and less messy for the dog to bite into and chew.

Most dogs prefer canned food, perhaps because it smells and tastes more like real meat than a bowlful of kibble. Canned food has a higher percentage of moisture (75 percent), making it a good source of water, but why pay for something you can get

Fats also enable the dog's body to absorb the fat-soluble vitamins, A, E, D, and K.

Carbohydrates provide energy too, but not in as concentrated a form as fats. Your Schip will get its needed starches and sugars from the carbohydrates in corn, rice, or wheat, which are included in commercial dog food formulas.

Vitamins and Minerals

Vitamins are organic substances essential for normal metabolic func-

from your kitchen tap? Some breeders add canned food, in small amounts, to dry kibble to encourage finicky eaters, but canned food requires refrigeration and is not suitable for free-choice feeding because, left out in the air, bacteria will contaminate it. Semimoist foods have less water than canned food but more than dry, and contain sugars and salts that help prevent the growth of bacteria. They usually are more expensive than dry food. Both canned and semimoist foods are not popular with Schipperke breeders for two simple reasons:

1. They don't help clean the Schips' teeth; and

2. Most breeders have more than one Schipperke at home, making it more economical and convenient (for storage, once opened) to buy good-quality dry food.

What's in a Label?

The ingredients listed on the back or sides of the label are arranged according to weight. The main ingredient in dry food, is usually poultry (chicken, chicken by-products, turkey, chicken meal) or corn. In canned foods, it's water, then meat products or corn. Next come the fats, preservatives, carbohydrates, vitamins, and minerals.

Choose a food with meat (chicken, beef, lamb, turkey, venison, or rabbit) as the top ingredient. This will ensure that your Schipperke receives the animal proteins that contain the necessary amino acids for good skin and coat.

Adjectives such as "natural" or "gourmet recipe," are usually an advertising copywriter's way to entice you to buy the product—they have no standardized meaning. Food with "no added preservatives" means that the dog food manufacturer hasn't supplied extra preservatives on top of the ingredients purchased from outside sources. No one food is 100 percent perfect for your individual Schipperke.

When buying food, look for the AAFCO statement.

Feed your puppy the food recommended by its breeder.

45

Follow your breeder's recommendation, and if, for some reason, that's not possible (for instance, if that brand isn't available in your area), buy a premium brand using the information in this chapter.

An adult Schipperke usually weighs between 12 and 18 pounds (5.4–8.2 kg), and this is often shown in the "toy breed and small dog" category on dog food labels. If your Schip gains weight on the recommended amount, feed less, unless of course, you have a growing puppy. If your dog is thin, you may have to feed more, but check with the breeder.

Some Schipperke lines mature late, remaining gangly for the first year or two. Common sense (and advice from your veterinarian or breeder) will help answer your questions about proper quantities and help you raise a healthy Schipperke.

Water, Water, All the Time

Without sufficient amounts, the cells in your Schip's body won't function normally and tissues will dehydrate. Water makes up more than half a dog's adult weight, and it should be available at all times to replenish excreted fluids. This means taking a water bottle or canteen for your Schip if you're on a long car trip, at a dog show, or spending an afternoon in the park. A thirsty Schip will drink from even the muddiest puddle, and stagnant water often contains disease-bearing organisms, which, at the very least, can give your Schip a bad case of diarrhea. The water bowl itself should be washed daily to prevent the incubation of germs and the formation of slimy residues. Of course, if you are trying to housebreak your Schipperke, remove the water at night.

Tip: Buy bottled water or bring water from home when traveling to areas with different water. Combine it gradually so the dog's system adjusts.

Feeding Your Puppy

One of the challenges in feeding a Schipperke puppy is to provide the high amounts of nutrients its little body needs without overfeeding it. Commercial balanced foods labeled "puppy formula" are available for this purpose. The Schip's breeder usually will send you home with a starter supply. Follow the breeder's guidelines for how much to feed, consult the label on the food bag, or ask your veterinarian. Since pups are individuals, the amounts will vary somewhat, but don't be surprised if your little Schip devours a cup (250 ml) of food a day.

An eight- to twelve-week old puppy should eat four times a day (if it's convenient for you, otherwise three times), but at the same time each day. For example, a pup eating one cup (250 ml) should receive four portions of one-quarter cup (62.5 ml) each. This is one of the reasons getting a puppy means a lot of work.

Your Schip should continue with three meals a day until it is nine months old, then it's fine to feed two meals daily. At 18 months you can go to one meal a day, although dividing the daily ration in half and feeding two meals is better for the dog's digestive system. If you feed dry food, you can feed free choice, allowing your Schipperke to eat as much or as little as it wants throughout the day (and night). However, if you have more than one animal, free-choice feeding probably won't work. Some Schipperkes will eat the cat's food as well as their own or try to steal kibble from your other dog or dogs. Also, you won't be able to tell if one dog isn't eating because it's impossible to monitor the food intake.

You can tell whether your pup (and adult dog) is being properly nourished by looking at its stools. The "leavings" should appear relatively small and firm but not dry, a sign that the Schip's body has digested all the nutrient-giving ingredients. If the stools are consistently loose, greasy-looking, or foul-smelling, consult your veterinarian at once.

Food for Adults and Seniors

Most Schipperkes start eating an adult or maintenance diet between the ages of 9 and 18 months. If you're feeding a brand that offers different formulas for the different life stages of a dog, after the "puppy or growth formula" you should switch to the "adult or canine maintenance" food. When you change, it's easier on the dog's digestive system to gradually add the new formula to the old over the course of a few days. Be sure to check the recommended amounts to feed, and then adjust them for your own Schipperke.

If you decide to change brands for the adult diet, follow the same "mix-it-in-gradually" method. Older Schipperkes should continue to eat the balanced adult diet, but monitor the amounts you feed so the dog doesn't become overweight. Your Schip needs to reduce if it *looks* fat. Do its sides bulge? Does it seem to waddle from excess weight? If you can't feel its ribs, your Schipperke is too fat, and you should cut back on the amount you are feeding without changing to a "diet" food. The so-called "lite" formulas may not provide the right amounts of proteins and fats to keep your Schipperke's coat in prime condition.

Special Formula Diets

Schipperkes, in general, are hardy little creatures that can eat a balanced, canine maintenance diet and thrive, but occasionally, a Schip may develop a food allergy, intestinal problem, or skin condition that requires a change in diet. Your veterinarian should examine the dog to determine if a special diet is necessary. If it is, be sure to follow the feeding instructions exactly as prescribed. Schipperkes

can look sulky and pathetic, making you think you're starving them to death. This may tempt you to throw some extra tidbits their way, but don't do it. Remember, your Schipperke's health depends on you.

Supplements

If you're feeding your Schipperke a well-balanced diet, there's no need to add "extras." In fact, supplementing can *unbalance* a scientifically formulated diet. If you overload your Schipperke with too many vitamins and minerals, you may cause a toxic build-up that can lead to health problems later on. Some manufacturers, to make up for nutrients lost through processing dog food, claim to add an extra (but not toxic) level of vitamins and minerals to compensate for this loss. A Schipperke that isn't eating (a rare phenomenon) and therefore isn't getting all the nutrients it needs, should be examined by a veterinarian.

Bones

Schipperkes love bones and will chomp on any they find, including chicken bones left behind by careless people eating outdoors. Chicken, poultry, and pork bones splinter easily, as do certain steak bones. They can pierce your Schip's throat, stomach, and intestines, causing death.

Some Schipperke owners avoid all bones because it's always possible that a piece could break off, leaving a sharp and dangerous segment behind. This is sound advice. If you do give your Schip a bone, choose a good, solid knucklebone from your butcher, and offer it to your Schipperke only when someone is home to check on it. After the "bone session" is over, pick up what's left to keep away insects, germs, and unwanted visitors such as stray dogs, raccoons, and rats.

Tip: You can buy safe, hard nylon bones or beef bones that have been

To keep your Schip fit and healthy, do not overfeed or overtreat.

in the Schip receiving a treat. But a Schipperke is a small dog, and it's best not to overdo the treats or it'll add unwanted weight. If you must give a treat (and I confess, *I* do), think small. Buy good-quality biscuits made for small dogs and feed one or two daily.

Your Schip will also enjoy low-fat cheese cut into small pieces, raw carrots, and other vegetables such as cooked squash and broccoli. Remember to keep the quantities small and *do not overfeed.*

Schipperkes adore liver, freeze-dried or fresh cooked, and this makes an excellent reward for training. But again, don't overdo it; liver is very rich and will cause your Schip to have loose stools. It.also contains high amounts of vitamin A, which should not be added to an already balanced diet.

Tip: Break big treats into small bits.

Chews, Pig Ears, and Other Animal Parts

Schips enjoy rawhide sticks or small, knotted rawhide bones, and they'll gnaw until the rawhide turns to mush, then swallow it. *Never leave your Schipperke alone with rawhide, and when it turns to mush, throw it away.* It can get caught in the throat as the dog tries to swallow it, and your Schipperke could choke to death. Pressed rawhide bones in different flavors and shapes are safer since they don't turn to mush.

Dried pig ears, plain or smoked, are another Schip favorite, but they are greasy and shouldn't be eaten on carpets or furniture. Cow hooves (the real thing) give a Schipperke hours of chewing pleasure, but they smell bad to humans, and are best eaten outdoors. Other dried animal parts, available at dog shows or through specialty distributors, include tracheas, stomachs, ligaments, and intestines. Hopefully, your Schip will be happy with ordinary rawhide.

heat sterilized. Both come in flavors and are available in pet shops, at dog shows, through pet product catalogs, and even in some supermarkets. Most Schipperkes enjoy them.

Treats

Schipperkes are born beggars. From an early age, most of them learn to stand on their hind legs and paw the air, looking adorable. This "pattycaking" melts human hearts and usually results

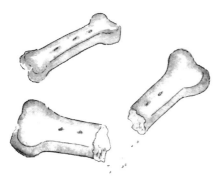

Feed small treats or break larger treats in pieces, but don't overfeed.

Your Schipperke's Health

Schipperkes, so far, have escaped many of the health problems afflicting more popular breeds. Although Schips are hardy dogs that don't need pampering, routine quality health care is important. This means vaccinating your Schip against common canine diseases, keeping it free of parasites, and taking it for regular veterinary checkups.

Vaccinations

Through their mother, puppies are born with a natural immunity to the most deadly canine diseases *if* the mother is properly vaccinated. This immunity wears off after weaning, when the pups no longer nurse from the dam and get protection from her antibodies, so vaccination becomes necessary. Your breeder's veterinarian most likely will have administered the first two sets of shots and it will then be up to you to have your veterinarian complete the series.
• CPI vaccine protects against canine distemper and measles.
• DHLPP combats distemper, canine hepatitis, leptospirosis, parvovirus, and parainfluenza.
• The first rabies shot (in countries where rabies exists) is given along with DHLPP at age 14–16 weeks.
• Other shots may be necessary depending on where you live.
Rabies and DHLPP are given regularly over the course of your Schipperke's life. Consult your veterinarian for scheduling.

Regular Checkups

The best way to make sure your Schipperke stays healthy is to visit your veterinarian on a regular basis. Puppies need more frequent attention. They require the balance of their shots, and they may pick up worms or diseases from other dogs. You and your veterinarian should agree upon what constitutes "regular checkups."

Helping Your Veterinarian

Write down your observations. Record frequency of symptoms where applicable:
• Appetite: Not eating?
• Behavior: Listless? Withdrawn? Snappish?
• Eyes: Any discharge? What color? Tearing? Redness of sclera?
• Ears: Odor? Discharge? Scratching? Head shaking?
• Mouth: Breath—Odor? Foaming? Champing? Vomiting?
• Nose: Discharge? Color? Dry? Warm? Cold? Moist?*
• Gait: Lameness? Which side? Skipping on one leg? Accidents?
• Lungs: Coughing? "Rattling" noises? Rapid breathing?
• Penis/Vagina: Discharge? Color?
• Stools: Color? Consistency? Blood?

*Noses usually are wet and cool. Warm and dry may mean fever. Take rectal temperature. Normal, adult temperature is 100–102.5°F (37.8–39.2°C).

49

1. Brain
2. Spinal cord
3. Stomach
4. Kidneys
5. Rectum
6. Bladder
7. Small intestine
8. Spleen
9. Liver
10. Diaphragm
11. Heart
12. Lungs
13. Esophagus
14. Thyroid gland
15. Trachea

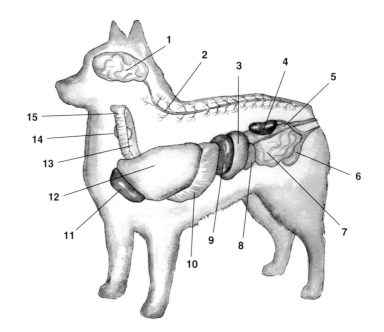

Regular veterinary checkups will ensure that your Schip's internal organs are working properly. In between visits, it's up to you to watch for signs of trouble.

Talking with Your Veterinarian

Veterinarians are at a disadvantage when it comes to treating their patients; obviously, animals can't explain where it hurts. Your Schip and your veterinarian will depend on you to describe, as well as possible, the symptoms that may require treatment. It's important to find a veterinarian who will, in addition to examining your dog, listen carefully, discuss the diagnosis, the options for treatment, and the cost. Your veterinarian should answer your questions, and you, in turn, should be ready to answer his or hers (see Helping Your Veterinarian on page 49 for guidelines). If your veterinarian is not familiar with Schipperkes, you can "break the ice" by giving a brief history of the breed.

Danger Signals

Veterinary attention is recommended for:
1. Weight loss
2. Sudden change or loss of appetite
3. Shortness of breath
4. Excessive thirst and frequent urination
5. Lump on or under the skin

External Parasites

Depending on where you live, your Schipperke may get fleas and ticks. These parasites feed on blood, and your dog provides a convenient host.

Ticks

Ticks attach themselves to the dog and feed until they swell to the size of a pea. Most ticks, such as the common dog tick, are easy to find and to remove, even before they reach this swollen state; however, the deer tick, carrier of Lyme disease, is small, about the size of a poppyseed. It is hard to find in the Schipperke's dense coat unless you check carefully. Ticks can transmit disease to humans—babesiosis, Lyme, and Rocky Mountain spotted fever, among them. (See pp. 33–34.)

Fleas

Fleas spend most of their lives off the dog, laying eggs in your carpet or yard. To wipe out fleas, you must treat both the dog and the premises. Most Schipperke breeders prefer a natural approach—bathing (dog shampoos and water are instant flea killers), keeping the dog away from flea-infested areas, and using the flea comb as opposed to dousing the dog with chemicals or pills. Nevertheless, it's important to know the types of flea-killing products available today, should you consider using any of them.

IGRs and IDIs are insect growth regulators and insect development inhibitors that keep fleas from maturing, but do not kill adults. These products are given to dogs as pills or infused into flea collars. They appear in foggers or sprays to kill fleas in the environment.

Adulticides kill adult fleas and are available as dips, shampoos, powders, sprays, and collars. They also come in single application vials that allow the insecticide to permeate the fatty layer of skin beneath the dog's coat. If you use any of these products on your Schipperke, make sure they are marked *safe for cats*. Many insecticides contain chemicals that are too strong for Schipperkes. Products with pyrethrins, which come from chrysanthemums, are usually the safest, but they don't have long-term action and must be reapplied frequently.

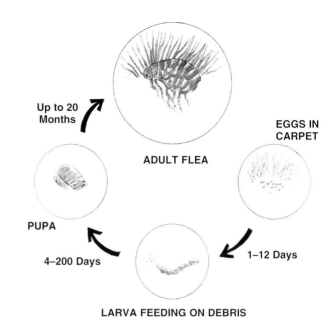

Up to 20 Months

ADULT FLEA

EGGS IN CARPET

PUPA

4–200 Days

1–12 Days

LARVA FEEDING ON DEBRIS

The Flea's Life Cycle.

Spraying your premises. Indoors, vacuum thoroughly before spraying. Dispose of the bag away from your home or you'll still have fleas. Use a commercial flea killer, available at garden shops, pet supply stores, or through catalogs, and be sure all dog toys, chews, and dishes are out of the way. Natural remedies, such as nematodes, which feed on flea larva, are safer, but if you have a large property, it can be costly to use them. You might establish a flea-free zone, an exercise pen (with high sides) in a shady spot until flea season is over.

City dwellers have a different problem. They can't spray the public parks where fleas breed, so they must keep their Schipperke out of grasses, bushes, and underbrush. If you notice your Schip's best dog friend scratching after a weekend in the country, assume it has fleas and take your Schipperke away, quickly.

Flea Allergy Dermatitis

Once bitten, some dogs react to flea saliva and suffer severe irritation around the hindquarters and anal area. Reddish bumps appear, and when scratched, become sores. Hair may fall out. If your Schipperke shows signs of this problem, see your veterinarian.

Worms

Most worms that afflict dogs are intestinal parasites. One exception is the heartworm, which is transmitted by mosquitoes. Adult worms, measuring four to twelve inches (10–30.5 cm) entwine around and throughout the heart. This eventually leads to heart failure. The best prevention is to put your Schipperke on a regular heartworm medicine that your veterinarian can prescribe.

Hookworms attach to the small intestine and suck blood. Dogs pick up larvae through contaminated soil or feces, and evidence can be seen in their stools. Puppies (even unborn and newborn) can contract a case of hookworms, but they are not usually seen in older dogs.

Roundworms are more of a threat to puppies than to adult dogs. A heavy infestation can cause death. Visual signs are a dull coat and a distended stomach, or a pot-bellied look. Vomiting, weight loss, diarrhea, with moving, white worms visible to the eye, are signs of roundworms. Pups can get roundworms by contact with soil harboring the eggs. Watch for frequent coughing and gagging, as worm larvae can find their way to the windpipe where they are swallowed.

Tapeworms are easy to detect. Dry, they look somewhat like a grain of rice. Alive, they resemble a strand of cooked spaghetti, which you might see dangling in the fur near your Schipperke's anus. The most common tapeworm is transmitted by fleas that the dog ingests while biting or licking its fur, but other sources include raw fish, raw meat, and dead animals. See your veterinarian if you suspect tapeworms.

Whipworms attach to the large intestine, and, because the female doesn't lay as many eggs as other worms, they may be difficult to detect in stool samples. Frequent stool checks may be needed in order for your veterinarian to make the right diagnosis.

Diseases and Ailments

Diarrhea

Diarrhea (loose, unformed or watery stools) can be caused by a variety of things—a change of diet or water, a worm infestation, or garbage gobbling, to mention a few. Most cases can be treated at home. Withhold food and water for 24 hours and give ice cubes to quench the dog's thirst. If there is no improvement after 24 hours, if vomiting and fever are present, or if there's blood in the stool, call your veterinarian.

Epilepsy

Epileptic seizures are triggered by the brain and can stem from bacterial infections in the brain, a head injury, or brain inflammation from distemper. Other forms are hereditary.

A seizure usually passes through three stages:
• In the first, called the *aura*, the dog may behave strangely, biting the air, sniffing in corners, staring blankly, foaming at the mouth, or shaking its head.
• In the next stage, the *rigid* phase, the dog collapses and twitches, throwing back its head and slobbering. It may lose bladder and bowel control. These two phases are over in less than five minutes.

• The third stage, *post-seizure*, may last several hours. During this time, the dog remains unsteady and confused. Any further upsets may trigger a new seizure.

If your Schipperke suffers a seizure, be sure to record everything you observe and inform your veterinarian at once. During the seizure, there is nothing you can do to help, other than cover the dog with a blanket and talk calmly to it. Keep your fingers and any other objects away from its mouth.

Epilepsy can be treated with drugs prescribed by your veterinarian. It may show up in a young Schipperke or not appear until age eight or nine.
Note: Schips have been known to literally knock themselves out, by running on a slippery floor and crashing into a wall, or banging into a tree trunk outdoors, then, a few months later, the dog may have a seizure. Therefore, it is important to keep track of all your Schip's accidents.

Hypothyroidism

The thyroid gland, located in the neck, regulates the dog's metabolism. When this gland produces insufficient amounts of hormones, hypothyroidism is the result. Dozens of breeds are susceptible to this condition, and among them is the Schipperke. Evidence of low thyroid usually appears after the dog is at least ten months old, or after puberty. Watch for these symptoms:
• thinning, sparse hair coat
• reddish cast to the coat (not to be confused with the rust color preceding the natural process of blowing coat)
• lethargy
• poor appetite (though many Schips remain active and hungry)
• loss of pigmentation on the nose, which may appear as a spot, and sometimes is misdiagnosed as a skin disease.

Behavior changes also can indicate a thyroid problem. Ask your veterinarian to do a blood test (T4) for thyroid. If the test comes back low or low-normal, your Schip should be put on daily thyroid supplements, which you can easily give with its meals.

Legg-Perthes

This disease afflicts small breed dogs, usually those weighing under 26.5 pounds (12 kg). It can occur between the ages of three months to thirteen months, though seven months is most common. Also known as aseptic necrosis and LCPD, (Legg-Calvé Perthes disease), it is caused by an inadequate supply of blood to the head of the femur, the thighbone that fits into the hip socket. The head or ball of this ball-and-socket joint wears away, causing lameness, and, though the dog outgrows the disease, the femoral head is left flattened and misshapen, generally corrected by surgery. There is no evidence that this is a hereditary disease, and many experts believe it stems from trauma such as jumping up and down on the rear legs.
Tip: Don't encourage your Schipperke to dance on its hind legs or jump from high places until its bones have finished developing.

Undescended Testicles

This condition is of concern only to people who plan to show or breed their Schipperkes. In the ring, males must have both testicles descended, and the judge will verify this by touching the dog. In the majority of puppies, testicles descend before birth but sometimes, this may not happen until age five or six months. At other times, testicles may retract back into the groin and then come down again. If testicles haven't descended by age six months (the age at which pups first may be shown), you should consult your veterinarian.

Exercising Your Schipperke

Schipperkes are active dogs. To stay fit and healthy, they must have exercise. Schips like to run, and if you're a jogger or a fitness walker, you've got a companion, but use common sense, adjusting distance and speed to weather conditions and your Schip's age. Try to give your Schip at least one energetic, long walk a day. If you let your Schip free in a fenced yard, it'll take care of its own exercise needs, especially if there are squirrels to chase. Puppies under six months require special consideration as their bones are still forming, and you must be careful not to stress them. Four walks a day with exercise chasing toys in the yard or house should be enough.

Hot Weather Precautions

The Schipperke's coat is a natural insulator in both cold and hot weather; therefore, you must never shave your Schip, thinking you're helping it stay cool. This will make it a target for stinging insects and fleas and is more apt to cause skin problems due to exposure. The black coat absorbs heat, and, along with the sun beating down on

Schips love cold weather, but when it's frigid, they can get frostbite on their pads and ears.

your Schipperke, can lead to heat stroke. If it's 80°F (26.7°C), it's too hot to leave a Schipperke outdoors.

Lifesaving tips:

• Never leave your dog in the car when it's 60°F (15°C) or hotter. Even in the shade with the windows partially open, (completely open allows a loose Schip to jump out or a passing thief to drop in), or on a cloudy day, a car will become dangerously hot and can result in the death of the dog.

• People who walk their Schips on the street and across blacktop roads should try to stay in the shade. These surfaces become extremely hot in the sun and can irritate your Schipperke's pads.

• Keep the water dish filled. If you go for a long walk, bring water in a plastic bottle or a special pet canteen. Use your spray bottle to dampen the coat while you're out.

Cold Weather Care

The Schipperke's coat acts like a down parka, with the undercoat trapping air and forming a warm layer next to the body. Schips don't require a wardrobe of doggie sweaters, nor do they need rain gear for wet weather, as the natural oils in the coat repel moisture. One good shake (followed by a rubdown from you) rids the coat of snow and rain.

Snow and ice can ball up under the feet, separating the toes and making it hard for the dog to walk comfortably. Keep pad hairs trimmed and use a pad protector cream or ointment, especially if there's salt on the ground. Some products are greasy and your Schip will leave paw prints on your floor or furniture if you don't wash the pads with warm water immediately upon returning home.

Dogs can get frostbite on the ears, toes, and, for intact males, on the scrotum. They are also subject to hypothermia—a serious drop in body temperature—when left in the cold for a long time, especially if the coat is wet. Cold, blustery winds can give your Schip a nasty cough if you leave the dog out for a long time. When it's extremely cold, it's best to limit outdoor exposure.

Note: Never let your Schip consume antifreeze—though it tastes good to dogs, it is a poison. Take the dog to the veterinarian *immediately* if the dog takes any!

Emergencies

Take a few minutes to set up a canine first aid kit, and make sure you have two very important numbers posted on or near your phones: your veterinarian's and the number of a 24-hour emergency animal clinic. Place these numbers in your car as well. Explain to everyone in your household the procedures for tackling emergencies.

Supplies to Have on Hand

• ball- (round) tipped scissors
• tweezers
• gauze (pads or rolls)
• absorbent cotton (not cosmetic puffs)
• hydrogen peroxide or special canine wound cleanser
• hydrocortisone ointment
• canine eye cleansing solution
• rectal thermometer (the digital type is safer than glass)
• antihistamine (pills* or liquid*)
• antidiarrheal medicine*
• muzzle (scarf, pantyhose, or leash may be used to make a muzzle)

Note: Reverse sneezing is a temporary, sudden condition that sounds as though your Schipperke is gasping for its last breath. This is thought to be a spasm of the throat muscles, perhaps due to mucus accumulation. You can stroke the dog's throat, but no treatment is necessary; the attack

*Check with your veterinarian for proper dose; write it down and tape to label.

An injured dog may bite. Make a quick muzzle from a scarf, leash, roll of gauze, or pantyhose.

In an Emergency

1. Clear breathing passages: open mouth, clear obstructions, pull tongue forward, breathe into nostrils 12–15 times per minute.
2. Keep dog calm; muzzle if necessary.
3. Call veterinarian.
4. Take action as described in the HOW-TO section that begins on page 56.

passes within a minute or two and the dog is fine.

Disaster Planning

Set up an emergency shelf in your cupboard for extra dog supplies in the event of a natural disaster such as a flood, hurricane, earthquake, tornado, or blizzard. This should include:
• food
• bottled water
• leash
• collar with ID tag
• a first aid kit
• canine life jacket (in flood zones)

Make one family member responsible for the Schipperke, so in the event of evacuation, there's no confusion about who has the dog. Always leash your Schipperke if you are forced to leave your home.

HOW-TO:
Handling Emergencies

Heat Stroke
Symptoms: Rapid, labored breathing, high body temperature, vomiting, collapse.

Action: Place the dog in cold water; cover it with cold, wet towels, or douse it with a garden hose.

Note: Many cases of heat stroke can be prevented if only dog owners would remember *to never leave their dog in the car in warm weather*.

Dog Bites
Action: Apply a muzzle; cleanse the wound with water and a canine wound cleanser. If bleeding, apply pressure, then cover with a bandage.

Tip: Watch the fur on your Schip's back, especially the ruff and the patch over the back near the tail nub. If it stands up (raised hackles), pull your Schip away from the other dog immediately—fights can erupt in a split second. Schips have been known to go after Airedales, Rottweilers, and other big game.

Serious Bleeding Wounds
Symptoms: Large amounts of blood, deep gash, puncture in head, chest, or abdomen.

Action: Cover the wound with a gauze pad and apply firm, direct pressure; add more dressing if blood soaks through. Cover any exposed internal organs with wet, warm sterile bandage, but do not try to push them back into place.

A collapsed ironing board forms a handy stretcher for transporting a Schip with a fracture. Position yourselves so the dog can't roll off.

• To control bleeding of the lower forelegs, apply pressure to the upper inside of the front leg.

• To control bleeding of the lower hind legs, apply pressure to the upper inside of the rear leg.

Shock
Symptoms: Labored or irregular breathing, dilated pupils, weak pulse, extremely pale gums. Shock may occur following serious injury or fright.

Action: Gently restrain the dog; keep it quiet and warm with head elevated.

Fractures
Symptoms: Inability to use the leg; pain.

Action: Apply a muzzle. Stem the bleeding (if present) and transport the dog to the veterinarian on a stretcher (use a board or any flat, inflexible surface). Do not attempt to set the fracture or pull it back into place.

Electrical Shock
Symptoms: Burns in the mouth (from chewing electrical cord); collapse.

Action: Do not touch the dog. Unplug the power source or separate the dog from the electrical source, using a wooden pencil, broom handle, or wooden spoon to push the cord away. Keep the dog warm. If unconscious and not breathing, perform artificial respiration: Place the dog on its right side, close its mouth, and exhale into its nose. Perform heart massage with your free hand (heart is in the lower half of the chest, behind the elbow of the left front leg). Place your hand over the heart and compress the chest one inch (2.5 cm). Do this six times. Wait five seconds to allow chest to expand, and repeat.

Burns
Symptoms: Blistering, singed hair, redness of the skin.

Action: Cool the burn with compresses soaked in cold water.

For burns, apply compresses soaked in cold water.

56

Poison

Symptoms: Diarrhea, vomiting, unsteadiness, convulsions.

Action: Identify the poison. Call the veterinarian or poison control center at once. Do not induce vomiting unless directed by the veterinarian.

Insect Bites

Symptoms: Swelling, itching, pain.

Action: Remove the stinger. Apply cold packs. Give proper dosage of an antihistamine.

Snakebites

Symptoms: Fang marks, pain, rapid swelling, weakness.

Action: Immediately take the dog to a veterinarian. If you plan to travel with your Schip to an area where there are snakes, check with your veterinarian *in advance*. Follow his or her advice regarding snakebites.

Choking

Symptoms: Difficulty in breathing, pawing at mouth, lips and tongue turn blue.

Action: Open the mouth and see if a foreign object is visible. Clear the airway by removing the object with tweezers, but be careful not to push it farther down the throat. If you cannot remove the object, place your hands on both sides of the dog's rib cage and apply firm,

quick pressure. Or you may lay the dog on its side and strike the side of the rib cage firmly with the palm of your hand three or four times. Repeat sequence until the object is dislodged. Call your veterinarian.

Note: If an object is removed from the throat but the dog still is not breathing, place the dog with its right side down. Close its mouth and exhale directly into the nose—not mouth—until the chest expands. (You may do this with a handkerchief or thin cloth over the nose, if you prefer.) Exhale 12 to 15 times per minute. At the same time, apply heart massage with the other hand. The heart is found in the lower half of the chest behind the elbow of the front left leg. Place your hand over the heart and compress the chest 1 inch. Apply heart massage 70–90 times per minute. Immediately call veterinarian.

Suffocation from Drowning

Note: Schips have been known to jump off boats into very deep water. If you plan to take your Schipperke boating, learn these techniques:

Action: Hold the dog upside down by the hind legs to allow water to run out. Next, position the dog with its head lower than its chest (roll a large towel to elevate the body) and begin artificial respiration.

For drowning emergencies, hold the Schipperke upside down by the hind legs to allow water to flow out. Then place the dog on the ground, with the head lower than the chest, and perform artificial respiration.

Note: Prevent trouble before it starts by always placing a canine life jacket on your Schip or by securing the dog to the boat with a lifeline.

57

Growing Old

It's hard to imagine your Schipperke will ever grow old and slow down. Bright-eyed and ever-curious, the breed typically looks healthy and strong even at ten or older, provided good care has been given over the course of the dog's life. Most Schips turn gray around the muzzle, then around the ruff, and some reddening of the coat may occur. Arthritis may set in, causing stiffness, and teeth, even with brushing, may turn yellow with age. Cataracts may develop after the age of ten, eventually leading to blindness if the dog lives another five or six years. Schipperkes have a life span of around 13 to 16 years, though there have been a few documented cases of them reaching their early twenties.

When your Schip grows old, you'll have to adjust food portions to suit a slower activity level. Schips tend to get pudgy if allowed to eat all they want without rigorous exercise, which of course, is not feasible for most old dogs.

Saying Good-bye

Sadly, though, there will come a time when you will have to part with your little friend, either because of disease or the decrepitude of old age. This will be one of the most difficult decisions you (and your veterinarian) will have to make. If you can keep your Schipperke comfortable so its life remains pleasant and it is still able to enjoy your company, then by all means do so. But if each day becomes an ordeal, then you owe the dog peace, through euthanasia.

Once the decision has been made to "put the dog to sleep," discuss plans for the remains—burial or cremation. In some areas, you can bury your pet in your yard. If you choose a pet cemetery, check its reputation carefully. In recent years, there have been scams involving some of these facilities. Inform all family members about the dog's condition and discuss the steps you are planning to take; do not lie to a child and say "Skippy ran away." Then make your appointment with your veterinarian.

Many veterinarians will come to your house and administer the injections, first a tranquilizer, then the shot that stops the heart, painlessly. Whether at home or at the animal hospital, if you can keep your composure, stay with your Schipperke, hold it, and talk softly as the veterinarian puts it to sleep.

Tip: Make arrangements now for your Schipperke's care in the event something happens to you. Many people stipulate this in their wills and put money aside for the dog. Others make arrangements with the breeder or a family member to take the dog in the event of a tragedy. Some, in prenuptial agreements, state what would happen to the dog in case of divorce. Taking action today will prevent your Schipperke from ending up in a shelter if trouble unexpectedly strikes.

Schipperkes on the Go

The Schipperke is one of the most eager canine travelers; say "boat ride" or "car" and your Schip's ears will perk up. In fact, your Schip's enthusiasm may cause you to let down your guard and relax the training ground rules you've worked so hard to establish. In travel, as in all other areas of your Schip's life, your job is to ensure the dog's safety and well-being.

Riding in Cars

If your Schip had its way, it would stand on the passenger's seat, front paws on the door, nose out the window, sniffing the breeze. Nothing could be more dangerous for a dog. First, dirt, seeds, and road dust could lodge in its eyes. But more seriously, a sudden stop or hit from the rear would throw the dog against the dashboard, resulting in severe injury or death. It may notice a squirrel on someone's lawn and, on an impulse, jump out the window, or the airbag could inflate and crush it. This is why your Schipperke must always travel in a crate. Loose, it may want to see what's happening on your side of the car, creating a serious hazard. Once in the crate, it'll settle down and sleep, enjoying the ride on *your* terms.

An impact-resistant, molded plastic, airline-approved carrier is your best choice. Be sure to add a pad or blanket for your Schip's comfort and secure the crate so it doesn't tip over on turns.

Traveling by Plane

Most Schips can fit into soft-sided pet carriers that slip under the seat.

The majority of airlines allow pets as long as they are in approved carriers, are in good health, and have a current rabies vaccination certificate. Check with the airline in advance to make sure you have the required health certificates. If you are traveling outside your national boundaries, call the consulate of your destination country and find out what health documents are required for the dog.

Your next step is to buy a soft-sided carrier. The hard plastic cabin kennels that fit under the seat are a tight squeeze for a Schipperke. When buying a carrier, buy the large size, and check the tag or label for a listing of airlines that accept that product for pet transport. If you plan to fly with an airline that's not listed, call and ask about its rules regarding dogs on board. You want your Schipperke to be in the cabin with you, if at all possible. Though airlines are striving to improve conditions in the baggage area where

Crated, your Schipperke is safe for automobile travel. Some crates have slots for the seat belt to pass through.

If your Schip is well-behaved, you may take it along to an outdoor café.

larger crated pets must travel, you'll enjoy peace of mind when your Schip is asleep in its bag, under the seat. Airlines usually restrict the number of pets on board in the cabin to one in first class and one in coach so, when making your reservation, tell them you have a small dog traveling with you. In the United States, this will generally add about $50 each way to the price of your ticket.

In the event you must ship your Schipperke in the hold, make all arrangements with the airline beforehand. Insist upon seeing the crate loaded onto *your* flight. Travel by night in hot weather or to hot weather destinations to cut down the dog's discomfort. Be sure to attach a spill-proof water container to the inside of the crate door. Affix "live animal" stickers on the crate (these come with airline-approved crates) and make sure identification stickers and tags are prominently displayed.

Remove the collar so it cannot catch on the crate door. Unfortunately, this also removes your dog's identification tag so you should have your Schipperke tattooed or microchipped in the event the crate opens in an accident, allowing the dog to escape. (see page 62 for details).

Taking the Bus or Train

On public transportation your Schipperke can travel in the soft-sided case, but on private bus lines, you may have to pay extra for your pet, and if you're planning a trip, you should call and ask. Usually, train lines and subways insist on a carrier. In any event, your Schipperke will be content as long as its traveling with its favorite companion—you.

Cabs or Car Services

Many drivers-for-hire dislike taking canine passengers. They think (wrongly) the dog will urinate in the car or leave messy tracks on the seat. These drivers have no idea how clean Schipperkes are, and what great passengers they make; but to avoid problems, it's best to put your Schip in the soft-sided carrier when taking a cab or car service.

In the City

Some cities are dog-friendly, providing outdoor runs where dogs can romp and socialize. In Paris dogs are welcome in cafés and restaurants. In New York City they may go shopping with you in certain department stores and join you at an outdoor café, but the health code prohibits them from entering food stores and restaurants. Cities have laws and you, as a responsible dog owner, should familiarize yourself with them and obey them.

"Pooper-scooper" and leash laws are the most common. Picking up after a Schipperke is easy. If you're feeding good-quality food, the dog will produce firm, small stools so all you need is a plastic bag; there's no need to buy fancy scoopers.

Most cities require you to keep your dog on a leash, but as a responsible Schipperke owner, you already do that. Be sure your Schip's collar has an identification tag, giving your phone number and the phone number of your veterinarian.

Schipperkes must be socialized to accept the variety of people (and dogs) they'll meet in a city. Though they instinctively are wary of strangers, you cannot allow your Schip to lunge at people or bark at them. Take the coin can with you on walks, if necessary. **Note:** If your Schipperke came from a breeder in the country, the sound of sirens and honking horns may be frightening. Don't coddle the pup or it'll think you're rewarding it for being fearful. Say in a cheerful tone, *"Let's go."* Use treats, if needed.

In the Suburbs and Country

No matter how far from the road your house may be, if you have a Schipperke, you need a fenced area. Natural curiosity will drive your Schip to examine every square inch of your yard, even if your "yard" is a ten-acre estate. Without boundaries, your Schip will continue its investigation, even though that might take it miles from home and into the path of danger. When outside, your Schipperke should always wear a buckle collar with an identification tag.

You also can protect your Schipperke by having it tattooed or microchipped, forms of permanent identification that can help speed a return to you if the dog ever dashes out of the house without its collar and tags (see page 62 for details).

Fences

Wood fences are an effective way to contain your Schipperke, provided the slats are close together, as in a stockade fence, to prevent escape. Schips like to dig; therefore, you must make sure the bottom of the fence is sunk deep enough into the ground to prevent your pet from digging under it.

Schipperkes love the outdoor life. Fence your yard to protect your dog.

Always check the fence for loose slats or evidence of chewing. If your Schip chews the fence, correcting the behavior by putting bitter apple or vinegar on the wood will save you from future costly repairs and the possibility of the dog's escape.

Always keep your Schipperke on a leash when you're out walking.

61

Schips are great athletes, and many can jump from the ground into the arms of a standing adult. Make sure your fence is high.

Chain link. Though not as attractive as wood, many are coated with black or dark green vinyl to blend in with the landscape. The same warnings apply: Sink the fence deep and make it high. Some Schipperkes have been known to scale a chain link fence and disappear over the top. If your Schip tries this, correct immediately with your voice or the coin can.

Buried wire containment systems or "electronic fences." Sold under various names, these systems employ an electromagnetically charged wire or radio wave, buried under ground, bordering the area you want "fenced." The dog wears a collar with a battery-powered receiver that picks up this signal. When the dog approaches the off-limits area, the collar gives off a warning beep. If the dog doesn't retreat, it receives a quick zap. Some companies send a trainer/installer to condition the dog to the signal and the zap. In other cases, you must train (and install the wire) on your own, but do not just put the collar on the Schipperke and expect it to know it's fenced in.

These systems can be effective with Schipperkes. But there are drawbacks: Loose dogs may enter your yard. Also, if your Schip runs through the field and gets zapped, very likely during the first weeks of use, it won't return to the yard because it'll get zapped coming back in. Use this system only if you can keep an eye on your dog.

No matter what type of fencing you choose, always remember that a bored Schipperke will seek adventure. When outside, give your Schip a tasty knucklebone or hard nylon bone to keep it busy, plus plenty of fresh water. If you have to go to the store or leave your premises, even for a short time, it's safest to put your Schipperke indoors, in the crate.

Never tie your Schipperke to a tree or stake. Tethered in one spot, the dog will try to find a way to escape, getting its legs tangled in the tie-out or possibly wrapping itself around the tree so tightly it chokes.

Microchip Identification

About the size of a rice grain, microchips are implanted beneath the scruff of the dog's neck by a veterinarian. Each chip has its own code number, linked to a database, which only a special scanner can detect. Microchipping doesn't hurt the dog, and it lasts a lifetime but not all veterinarians and animal shelters have scanners, and those who do may have devices that can't read your particular chip. Also, unless your Schip wears a tag noting the presence of a microchip, no one but a veterinarian or shelter equipped with a scanner will know it's there. Consult your own veterinarian about microchipping.

Tattoo Registry

Many Schipperke breeders have their dogs tattooed with an identifying number on the inner thigh or underbelly. This is done by a veterinarian or experienced canine tattooer. The tattoo number should be registered with a national pet registry; otherwise, a finder won't know how to return the dog to you. Many people use their Social Security numbers, which only works *if* you sign on with a registry. The Social Security agency will not provide information regarding the number to a person finding your dog. However, a tattoo may discourage a thief. In the United States, laboratories, by law, may not use tattooed dogs for research. (See Useful Addresses and Literature, page 75, for addresses of microchip and tattoo registry.)

None of these systems is 100 percent foolproof, but they will increase your chances of getting your Schipperke back, should you ever become separated.

Dual-Home Schips

Some lucky Schipperkes live in a city apartment during the week and have a country place for weekends. If your Schip leads this happy life, it's wise to establish a relationship with a local veterinarian, explain your lifestyle situation, and find out what, if any, additional vaccinations your Schip might need for that area. Be sure your Schipperke has identification tags for both city and country.

On the Water

Some Schipperkes like to swim, others puddle around by the shore, but few can resist a boat ride. Black dogs need extra protection from the sun since their coats readily attract and absorb heat, which can lead to heatstroke. If you're taking your Schip on a boat, pack your spray bottle and keep the coat damp. Bring drinking water and a bowl. To retard coat reddening, use a sun-block made for dogs and be sure there's a shady spot on the boat for your Schip to rest. You can create a comfortable spot using a sun-reflecting "space blanket."

Never assume your Schip can swim to shore. Always use a canine life jacket, available through catalogs or pet supply shops. If you have a swimming pool, do not let your Schipperke have access to it. Dogs sometimes jump in, but often are unable to find their way out. Be sure to rinse off all salt water and pool water to prevent

If you take your Schip boating, provide water, shade, and a canine life jacket. Learn first aid for drowning and safety drills for "Schip overboard!"

skin problems such as itching, flaking, and coat discoloration.

Using a Dog Walker

Dog walking services offer a way for your Schipperke to get out for exercise and potty when you can't take the dog yourself. It's important to meet the person who will walk your Schip and introduce the dog to that person. Find out how many dogs are walked in the pack and what kind, and ask how long the walk lasts.

Agree on how much you'll pay for how many walks per week, and if possible, get it in writing. Since Schips are wary of strangers, and some might be aggressive toward an "intruder" entering the home, make sure the Schip and the dog walker get along.

Always leave your veterinarian's phone number in a prominent place.

HOW-TO:
Understanding Your Schipperke

Two strong instincts govern your Schipperke: the watchdog attitude and the rat-catcher/hunter's instinct. These are in your Schipperke's genes, and have been for several hundred years. You cannot change what's natural, but by understanding why your Schipperke behaves in a certain way, you can guide it to behave in ways that'll please you as well as the people the dog will meet during its lifetime.

Any strange noise will alert your Schipperke to protect your home by barking.

The Watchdog Attitude

Schipperkes bark first and ask questions later. While this is an excellent trait, it must be controlled or you will find yourself being "warned" about every noise in the neighborhood.

As your puppy or new adult dog adjusts to life in your home, it may bark less at sounds it hears every day. This depends on the individual dog. Help your Schipperke be a good neighbor as well as a good watchdog by using key training words like "Enough" after the Schip has given the first warning barks.

Company's coming. Schips don't distinguish between first-time and long-time visitors; both get the watchdog treatment. Train your Schip to accept guests. Never let your Schipperke jump on people. Nails, even short ones, can tear a hole in a silk skirt or panty-hose.

Catching Rats

The Schip's desire to catch small game is much stronger than its desire to be a good dog and remain at your side. Always keep a tight hand on the leash, even when stopping to chat with a friend, in case your Schip sees a squirrel to chase.

Schipperkes also will go after geese, raccoons, and foxes. They've even been known to dive off a dock to catch jellyfish. Never give your Schip a chance to interact with these creatures. It can only cause harm.

Lapdogs

Schips look so cuddly that people naturally want to hug them, but often the Schip won't cooperate. Some will stand on your lap for petting, but not lie there. Others will sit beside you and let you pet them until they get bored. Some *will* snuggle on your lap and relax for a while and many will demand affection by putting their paws

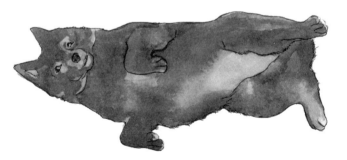

Schips often lie on their backs, not for submission, but to nap or to get you to stop what you're doing and scratch their bellies.

on your arm or nuzzling your hand. It depends on the Schip's individual personality; it is not a function of gender.

Expression and Body Language

"Aren't I cute?" backroll. In most breeds, lying on the back is a sign of acute submission, but with the Schipperke, it can be a way to get attention. You may be working at your computer, when suddenly you look down and see your Schip on its back. Notice the eyes. It's watching you, hoping you'll leave what you're doing and play or scratch its belly. This position is also a favorite for naptime.

Doorstop. Your Schipperke may plunk down across the threshold of your bedroom or bathroom while you're dressing to go out. Undoubtedly, it will have lost its alert and watchful expression. Some owners become alarmed, thinking their Schip might be ill. It isn't—it wants to go with you. Once you put it in its crate, it'll settle down and take a nap.

Pattycake. Some Schips are born knowing how to stand on their hind legs and paw the air, or pattycake. Some can be taught: others may not do it at all. Schips pattycake when they want attention, treats, or when you ask them to show off.

Other signals. When you reprimand your Schipperke for misbehavior, the ears will flatten against the head, then perhaps move up and down in a fluttery motion. The dog may

When relaxing or acting as a "doorstop," Schips often assume the frog position.

slink instead of walking upright. This is normal. After a reprimand it's best to let 15 to 20 minutes go by before you "make up." When you do, pat your Schipperke once or twice, but don't get too emotional.

An Energetic Athlete

Schipperkes are fast. They can turn on a dime and change direction, jump up to catch a Frisbee, or leap off a grooming table in a flash. When they run in circles, you'll swear their body is sideways parallel to the ground. Schips have a catlike grace, and though they can't climb trees, it doesn't stop them from trying when hunting squirrels. Do Schipperkes ever sleep? Yes. Do they ever run out of steam? Usually, when they reach old age.

When reprimanded, a Schipperke's alert stance collapses.

Organized Fun and Competition

Since Schipperkes always are eager for new adventure, you might consider entering yours in a dog show. Even if your Schip isn't perfect-looking, meaning you can't show in Conformation, there are other types of shows that are fun.

Conformation

This is the "breeders' class." The purpose is to show those dogs whose attributes best represent the breed as depicted in the standard, and therefore are most likely to reproduce dogs of their own or better quality. These Schips must not be neutered or spayed, and males must have both testicles descended. Dogs and bitches (from puppies to "unfinished" or still-to-be champion adults) are judged in their respective classes according to each trait described in the standard, among them: eyes, ears, head, bite, coat pattern, expression, gait, and temperament. In the United States, to become a champion, a dog or bitch must be awarded 15 points. Two sets of these must be majors—a win earning three to five points, depending on the number of Schips competing, and they must be won under two different judges.

Once a champion, your Schip may enter the Best of Breed class. If it wins, the next step is Group where it competes against the winners of each of the non-sporting group breeds—Dalmatians, French Bulldogs, Poodles, and Tibetan Spaniels, to name a few. Dogs in this group are those that are no longer used for their original purposes. For example, Poodles once were hunting dogs and Dalmatians, coach dogs.

At AKC-sanctioned shows, there are seven groups: Sporting, Hound, Working, Terrier, Toy, Non-sporting, and Herding. If your Schip wins first place (Group I), it goes on to try for Best in Show against each winner of the remaining six groups.

Conformation Schips are shown on a skinny show lead, and must know how to pose or "stack" on a table so a judge can examine them. They learn quickly because in conformation, treats can be used to bait the dog and keep it interested.

Most Schipperkes are owner-handled, but this looks easier than it is. Before setting foot in the show ring, it's best to take handling classes with your Schip. Sometimes obedience training schools also offer handling classes, but if there are none in your area, you will have to attend dog shows and try to find a Schipperke owner-handler who will give you some pointers or become your mentor.

Many champions in the United States also have their Canadian championships and carry the title Am. Can. Ch. (American Canadian Champion) before their names. In Canada, dogs need ten points to become champions, and there is no requirement for majors.

Obedience

This is a challenge for Schips because their curiosity about their surroundings will overshadow any desire to listen to you. And that is the trick. *You* need to figure out how to get and keep your Schipperke's attention during the exercises on which the judge will rate you. While training, this is easy; you can use treats. But in the ring, treats are not allowed.

Obedience entails executing certain actions on command. To earn a CD (Companion Dog), the most basic title, your Schip must earn a qualifying score in a variety of exercises, among them heeling on lead, walking a figure eight, allowing a judge to examine it while standing, heeling off lead, and sitting for one minute and staying down for three minutes in a group that often is packed with big dogs such as Rottweilers and Dobermans.

A dog needs three qualifying scores or "legs," earned at three different shows, under three different judges, to get the title. Other obedience titles, in order of ascending difficulty are: CDX (Companion Dog Excellent), UD (Utility Dog), UDX, (Utility Dog Excellent). The OTCh. (pronounced *ahtch*), Obedience Trial Champion, is the title awarded to dogs that have earned their UD and that have placed first in various trials in accordance with AKC rules.

The best way to prepare for any obedience title is to attend classes with your Schip. Sitting for a full minute next to a German Shepherd Dog or Boxer is a lot different than doing a long *sit* in your backyard.

Many Schipperkes that are champions go on to earn obedience titles. Ch. precedes the dog's name, and the obedience title comes after it.

Agility

If ever a sport were made for Schipperkes, agility is it. The variety of course obstacles—seesaw, weave poles, tunnel, hanging tire, broad jumps, and hurdles (adjusted to small dog height)—appeals to the Schip's curiosity and athletic ability. Agility lets you works as a team—your Schipperke navigates the course while you run alongside, directing. Titles your Schip can earn, each presenting a greater challenge over the one preceding, include NAD (Novice Agility Dog), OAD, (Open Agility Dog), ADE (Agility Dog Excellent), and MAX (Master Agility Dog). Many dog-training schools now offer agility classes since the sport continues to grow in popularity.

Tracking

Your Schip can become a canine Sherlock Holmes and sniff for "clues," articles dropped along a predetermined route by a tracklayer. In these competitions, dogs can earn TD (Tracking Dog), TDX (Tracking Dog Excellent), VST (Variable Surface Tracking), and CT (Champion Tracker), the last one reserved for dogs that have all three titles.

Canine Good Citizen (CGC)

Developed by the AKC to promote well-mannered dogs that can mingle with people and other dogs on city

Schips love the challenge of agility courses.

A Schipperke being shown in conformation must know how to stand quietly on a table, then move on the ground with flair.

Schipperkes are guaranteed to bring a smile to the sick or the injured. To work as a therapy dog, your Schipperke must possess sound temperament and flawless behavior.

streets as well as suburban sidewalks, the CGC challenges your Schip to walk with you on lead, around dogs and people without barking, pulling, or showing aggression, then to sit, calmly accepting a brief examination by a judge, to refrain from jumping on you and others, and to not misbehave when someone greets you. Canine good citizen tests sometimes are offered at dog shows and matches or at special events sponsored by organizations such as the ASPCA.

Therapy Dogs

Hospitalized children, the elderly, and those suffering from mental illnesses are among the humans who benefit from close contact with animals. A well-behaved, friendly dog that doesn't mind being petted can bring joy to these people. Though Golden Retrievers and Yellow Labs are among the most popular therapy dogs, there's no reason why a well-socialized, mature Schipperke wouldn't be able to perform this valuable service. In the United States, contact the Delta Society (425-226-7357) for information.

Other Shows

Matches offer a chance to practice for conformation point shows, obedience trials, and agility. Some are informal "fun" matches and others are sanctioned matches that are still informal, but governed by AKC rules. Either type provides a good learning experience for everyone—puppies, owner-handlers, judges, and stewards. Contact a kennel club in your area to find out about upcoming matches. Entries usually are taken the day of the match and the cost is minimal.

Point shows require advance entry at least three weeks before the event, and the cost, usually around $22, is much higher than the fees for matches. To enter, you need a premium list containing the official entry form, available from the show superintendent. Check dog magazines, the AKC, or your national kennel club for addresses and phone numbers. Point shows offer your Schip a chance to earn points toward a title in conformation, obedience, or agility. But not all shows offer all these disciplines. Check the premium list before you enter.

The Westminster Kennel Club Show in New York City along with **Crufts, in Birmingham, England,** are world-class shows, attracting thousands of spectators and exhibitors every year. Crufts, the largest dog show in the world, takes place in the spring, spans four days, and has an entry of over 20,000 dogs. Westminster is held over two days each February and, unlike Crufts, is reserved exclusively for champions. The breeds must be recognized by the AKC. Only 2,500 dogs are accepted, all vying for the coveted title, Best in Show. Over eight million people watch this dog show on television, and it draws a crowd in excess of 10,000 people each day.

The World Dog Show takes place in a different country every year. It includes all of the best-known breeds, and some of the rarest, and is fun to attend as a spectator or an exhibitor. First-time exhibitors abroad can minimize stress by making arrangements through a travel agency that specializes in dog-related travel.

The Schipperke's natural curiosity about its surroundings makes obedience training a challenge.

Breeders and Breeding

For every person who understands the true reason for breeding, there are thousands who think they ought to try it for fun, for money, or because their dog is "AKC." Millions of unwanted dogs are put down or euthanized every year. The victims are not only mixed-breeds; Schipperkes and other purebreds also meet this sad fate. The only reason to breed a Schipperke, or any other purebred dog, is to improve the breed by trying to produce quality pups of good health, sound temperament, and physical attributes that resemble the standard. This is done by serious people who study bloodlines and show their Schipperkes in competition. Most of them have a breeding program that looks ahead to the next 20 years.

Deciding to let your Schip have just one litter, or be a stud just one time, is unwise. This chapter explains why.

Altering Your Schipperke

Unless you're planning to show your Schipperke in conformation, the best course of action is to have it spayed or neutered. Spaying removes the reproductive organs of the female; neutering removes the testicles from the male. These are routine surgical procedures, and many animal clinics, recognizing the problem of pet overpopulation, offer low-cost spaying and neutering.

Unneutered male Schipperkes are more likely to get prostate trouble as they mature and will act more aggressively toward other unneutered males. Unspayed females may develop breast cancer, and when in season, will have to be confined. Even so, loose male dogs will prowl near your home, howl, cry, and try to find a way to get at the female.

Spaying and neutering generally take place when the dog is about seven months old, but a new trend is to alter much younger puppies, sometimes as early as eight weeks old. Check with your breeder and veterinarian to find out what's best for your Schipperke.

Note: Spayed and neutered dogs are welcome in obedience and agility.

Ethical vs. Unethical Breeders

An ethical breeder brings new Schipperkes into the world for one reason: to try to improve the breed. They will sell as pets those pups that may not mature in keeping with their breeding goals. They will not sell puppies to wholesalers, laboratories, or other outlets where a personal relationship can't be maintained and developed with the puppy's buyer. And they will take out of the breeding program any dogs or bitches that have "hereditary faults and disqualifying defects." An ethical breeder takes responsibility for each and every Schipperke he or she brings into this world.

An unethical breeder is someone who takes a male and a female and puts them together with no thought behind it. This type of individual doesn't know and doesn't care about bloodlines or the risk of passing on hereditary health problems. An unethical breeder often breeds a bitch every time she comes into season, an unhealthy practice for both mother and pups. Then a novice buyer sees an advertisement, wants

a Schipperke, thinks they look cute—
and Schipperke puppies do—buys
the dog, and gets a slew of health or
behavior problems several months
later. This can only lead to heart-
break, but the unethical breeder
doesn't care. He or she already is
breeding the next litter of genetically
inferior Schipperkes.

An ethical breeder doesn't breed his
or her bitch every time she comes into
season; therefore, he or she may
have a waiting list for puppies. Try to
be patient or ask for a referral to
another breeder. It is better to wait for
a puppy whose health and bloodlines
are guaranteed than to take a chance
on an unknown kennel that advertises
"Puppies for sale. All breeds. Custom
orders welcome."

Papers

Many novices believe that a dog
with papers is of special quality, but
papers, or registration papers, are
only what their name implies: They
show your dog is registered with the
kennel club that sanctions dog shows
and other dog events in your country.
In the United States, the AKC is the
most widely known registry. Even
dogs from puppy mills can have
"papers." Pet-quality dogs from reputable breeders have papers, though
many breeders offer only limited registration, which means the dog cannot
be shown and any offspring of that
dog or bitch cannot be registered.

The AKC, a nonprofit organization,
routinely registers the purebred offspring of the more than 140 breeds it
recognizes. All you have to do is send
in your fee and fill out the form correctly. Papers have no bearing on the
quality or health of the dog, nor do
they mean the dog is suitable breeding stock. So, if someone suggests
you breed your pup to theirs because
you both have "papers," you can see
why the answer should be No.

Breeding Is Risky Business

Since Schipperkes are not among
the top 20 most popular breeds, it
could take time to find good homes for
your litter. When you figure your costs
for veterinary care, shots, whelping
supplies, stud dog fees, prenatal care
of the mother, and showing, to develop
your reputation—if you're lucky enough
to produce at least one show-quality
pup—you can understand why, after
five years, most people who try breeding Schips, quit. Here is an overview of
what breeding entails.

Preparation

In the dog world, all are *not* equal.
Top-winning bitches mate with top-
winning or champion-producing studs
of the desired bloodlines. Ethical
breeders want to make sure that their
efforts, and the efforts of all those con-
scientious breeders who came before
them, are not undone by people who
mix the wrong genes.

Breedings normally are governed by
written contracts in which everything is
detailed, including stud fees and what
happens if your bitch doesn't conceive

1. Name
2. Breed
3. Color
4. Sire
5. Dam
6. Breeder
7. Number
8. Sex
9. Date of Birth
10. Date Certificate Issued
11. Your Name and Address

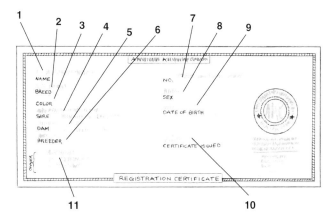

"Papers" merely refers to a dog's registration certificate. The term does not reflect on the dog's quality or health.

If you breed a litter, can you be sure none of your Schipperkes will end up in an animal shelter?

mating takes place. The female will flag the male by swishing her rear from side to side and exposing her vulva. She will stand for, or accept, a male during this six- to twelve-day period. If the bitch conceives, the puppies usually will be born between 58 and 65 days later.

The Stud

You must make all arrangements for the services of a stud dog months in advance of the time the bitch will come into season. It's wise to have the stud's sperm quality checked to make sure it is potent. Some first-time bitches may growl or snap at the stud. A first-time stud, overly eager, may ejaculate before penetration. Human hands may have to hold the stud and bitch in position to guide penetration and ensure the tie, the point at which sperm is ejaculated.

The Whelping Box and Supplies

About a week before puppies are expected, prepare your supplies:
• a rectal thermometer
• towels and washcloths
• newspapers (black ink only; color is poisonous to pups)
• heating pad and puppy box to keep the first pups born from getting chilled
• sterilized blunt-end scissors
• dental floss or sterile heavy silk thread (not cotton: it absorbs and retains moisture)
• sterile surgical gloves
• pediatric bulb syringe
• tube feeder
• emergency phone numbers
• bitch's milk replacement
• a small scale
• a pen and note pad for recording birth information.

The whelping box is the delivery room and nursery. It should be large enough for the bitch to comfortably lie on her side with the pups nursing in front of her, and low enough for her to step in and out without scraping her

or if the puppies are stillborn. There are false pregnancies where the bitch appears and acts pregnant but isn't. Sometimes the bitch reabsorbs the litter before they are born. In breeding only one thing is certain: Breeders face many problems before the first puppy is whelped.

The Heat Cycle

Some time after her six-month birthday, usually a few months later for Schipperkes, a female will come into season. This estrus, or heat cycle, will occur every six months after that, though it may vary from bitch to bitch, with some having longer times in between. The cycle lasts for approximately 21 days from the onset of vaginal bleeding. During the first six to nine days, the vulva will swell, and males, smelling special secretions in the bitch's urine, will become attracted; however, the female at this stage is not receptive and will growl at or bite a suitor. It is in the next phase, the standing heat, that

Sample Puppy Vaccination Schedule

(Note: Ever-changing research discoveries and new vaccines make it essential that you check with your veterinarian for the latest vaccination information for your area.)

Age	Vaccination
Six weeks	Distemper, Hepatitis, Parvovirus, Parainfluenza*
Nine weeks	Repeat series, plus Coronavirus
Twelve weeks**	Repeat nine-week shots

*Schipperkes may have an adverse reaction to the Leptospirosis vaccine, which is part of this series (DHLPP). If required, it's best to wait until age 3 months or older.
**Most breeders sell their pet puppies between 10 and 12 weeks.

nipples. A sturdy cardboard box, thickly lined with newspapers, with one end cut down for exiting, is fine as long as the low end is high enough to keep the puppies from escaping. The box must be kept clean, dry, and warm to ensure the health of the puppies and dam.

Keep an eye on the bitch as her time approaches (around the 58th day of the pregnancy), even if it means staying up all night—puppies whelped outside the box may not be found until it's too late. Be aware that whelping is messy business, with afterbirths, blood, and other fluids that must be wiped up to keep the area germ-free.

Caring for Newborns

You should plan to take at least two weeks off from whatever you're doing to care for your newborn litter. This is a time when you'll get little or no sleep because you'll constantly need to check on the puppies. Puppies must be kept warm in a room at a temperature of at least 70°F (21.1°C). A hot water bottle, a heating pad, or an infrared lamp are good sources as long as they cannot accidentally become too hot.

Tails and dewclaws are removed when the pups are three or four days old. Many veterinarians are unfamiliar with the correct tail-removing surgery, or in some cases, banding, for Schip-

perkes. Unlike Cocker Spaniels, no stump or protrusion should be visible. (If you live in Belgium or the United Kingdom, you won't have to worry; there, tail docking is no longer allowed.)

During the first two days after whelping, make sure all pups are nursing. This is when they receive colostrum through the dam's milk, which provides disease-fighting antibodies until it's time for their first shots.

If the puppies aren't nursing, you may have to hand-feed them with a commercial formula. Weigh the pups daily. Weight loss is a danger sign. A pup losing ten percent of its body weight may not survive.

Puppies need to be socialized and stressed in order to develop positive personalities. Experienced breeders know how to do this correctly.

Socializing Your Puppies

Before you sell your puppies, you must teach them how to cope with a variety of situations: being separated from littermates, traveling in a car (crated, of course), or loud noises such as vacuum cleaners or dishwashers. Puppies need to be stressed to a certain degree so they develop healthy, positive personalities. A fearful, quivering pup will not attract a buyer's eye nor will it grow up into a well-adjusted companion. Have your pups wear puppy collars—a different color for each one so you know who's who—and get them used to trailing a lead around the house or yard, under your watchful eye. But do not expose them to strange dogs or other animals because they will not have had all their immunization shots.

Note: You will need someone to evaluate your litter to help you decide your selling price. Evaluators usually are other established breeders or experts familiar with Schipperkes.

Finding Qualified Buyers

Reputable, established breeders often have waiting lists but you, as a novice, are an unknown. People who have researched the breed may not come to you, because they know the best way to get a Schipperke, either pet or show quality, is to contact an established breeder. Newspaper ads will bring a variety of "tire kickers" to your door, mostly people who don't understand the breed, but who are attracted by the rare-sounding name, Schipperke. The same holds true for cyberspace. Perhaps your friends are your best bet, the ones who claim they'd love to have one of your puppies. Ask them for a deposit well before the litter is born, something equivalent to $50, to determine how seriously they want one.

Once your puppies are sold, your responsibility as a breeder continues. New owners will have questions about care, training, and health checkups. You may have a pup returned if it has health problems, if you sold it with a health guarantee, as a reputable breeder should.

Homeless Schipperkes on the Rise

Every year, it seems, more and more Schipperkes turn up in shelters or get rescued from puppy mills. People often "get rid of" their Schips because they can't live with the dog's high activity level. Or they hate the barking. Or the dog chewed the rug or messed in the house. These people never should have owned a Schipperke in the first place. If you breed a litter, can you be sure your Schipperkes won't end up abandoned, in a shelter? Are you willing to take back a Schip you've bred, at any stage of its life, no matter what? And finally, do you really feel it's necessary to add more pups to the Schipperke, and to the total dog, population?

The Best Way to Learn About Breeding

Breeding requires an immense amount of dedication, time, and expense. In the United States, attend the Schipperke National Specialty, which takes place once a year in different states (contact the SCA for details). At a specialty show you will see over 200 Schipperkes and have a chance to meet dedicated breeders. Plan to devote several years to learning. Read books on genetics and breeding. Scour dog magazines for informative articles. If possible, form a relationship with an established breeder who will be your mentor, and try to learn *everything* possible about breeding Schipperkes.

Before bringing new dogs into the world, the most responsible people get educated first and breed later, if at all.

Useful Addresses and Literature

Clubs and Organizations

Schipperke Club of America
Call AKC Customer Service
  Call Center: 919-233-9767
  for name and phone number
  of current secretary.

American Kennel Club
51 Madison Avenue
New York, NY 10010
212-696-8200

United Kennel Club
100 East Kilgore Road
Kalamazoo, MI 49001-5598
616-343-9020

Canadian Kennel Club
100-89 Skyway Avenue
Etobicoke, ONT. M9W 6R4
Canada
416-675-5511

Periodicals

The SCA Bulletin
(call SCA secretary)

AKC Gazette
Subscriptions: 919-233-9767

Dog Fancy
P.O. Box 53264
Boulder, CO 80323-3264
1-800-365-4421

Dog World
P.J.S. Publications
2 News Plaza
P.O. Box 1790
Peoria, IL 61656
1-800-361-8056

Your Dog (newsletter)
P.O. Box 420272
Palm Coast, FL 32142-0272
1-800-829-5116

Video

Schipperke #WT 309
American Kennel Club
Attn: Video Fulfillment
5580 Centerview Drive, #200
Raleigh, NC 27606
919-233-9767

Tattoo and Microchip Registries

HomeAgain Companion Animal
  Retrieval System
(Registers Microchips and
  Tattoos)

AKC Companion Animal
  Recovery
5580 Centerview Drive, #250
Raleigh, NC 27606-3394
1-800-252-7894 or
1-800-2FIND-PET

InfoPET
(registers microchipped pets)
415 W. Travelers Trail
Burnsville, MN 55337
1-800-INFOPET

PETtrac
(registers pets implanted with
  the AVID microchip)
AVID
155 Woodside Drive
Mandeville, LA 70448
1-800-434-AVID

National Dog Registry
(registers tattooed dogs)
P.O. Box 116
Woodstock, NY 12498
1-800-NDR-DOGS
www.natldogregistry.com

Tattoo-A-Pet
6571 SW 20th Court
Ft. Lauderdale, FL 33317
1-800-828-8667
www.tattoo-a-pet.com

Books

Benjamin, Carol L., *Mother Knows Best: The Natural Way to Train Your Dog*. New York: Howell Books, 1985.

Carlson & Giffin, *Dog Owner's Home Veterinary Handbook*. New York: Howell Books, 1980.

Cecil & Darnell, *Competitive Obedience Training for the Small Dog*. Council Bluffs, IA: T9E Publishing, 1994.

Fogle, Bruce, *The Dog's Mind: Understanding Your Dog's Behavior*. New York: Howell Books, 1992.

Nichols, Virginia, *How to Show Your Own Dog*. Neptune, NJ: TFH Publications, 1970.

Rutherford & Neil, *How to Raise a Puppy You Can Live With*. Loveland, CO: Alpine Publications, 1992.

Schipperke Club of America, *The Complete Schipperke*. New York: Howell Books, 1993.

Appendix

Official Standard for the Schipperke

General Appearance

The Schipperke is an agile, active watchdog and hunter of vermin. In appearance he is a small, thickset, cobby, black, tailless dog, with a fox-like face. The dog is square in profile and possesses a distinctive coat, which includes a stand-out ruff, cape and culottes. All of these create a unique silhouette, appearing to slope from the shoulders to croup. Males are decidedly masculine without coarseness. Bitches are decidedly feminine without overrefinement.

Any deviation from the ideal described in the standard should be penalized to the extent of the deviation. Faults common to all breeds are as undesirable in the Schipperke as in any other breed, even though such faults may not be specifically mentioned in the standard.

In profile the Schipperke's silhouette is unique. (This is an artist's interpretation and is not meant to be construed as officially part of the written standard.)

Size, Proportion, Substance—*Size*—The suggested height at the highest point of the withers is 11–13 inches for males and 10–12 inches for bitches. Quality should always take precedence over size. ***Proportion*—**Square in profile. ***Substance*—**Thickset.

Head—Expression—The expression is questioning, mischievous, impudent and alert, but never mean or wild. The well-proportioned head, accompanied by the correct eyes and ears, will give the dog proper Schipperke expression. ***Skull*—**The skull is of medium width, narrowing toward the muzzle. Seen in profile with the ears laid back, the skull is slightly rounded. The upper jaw is moderately filled in under the eyes, so that, when viewed from above, the head forms a wedge tapering smoothly from the back of the skull to the tip of the nose. The stop is definite but not prominent. The length of the muzzle is slightly less than the length of the skull.
***Eyes*—**The ideal eyes are small, oval rather than round, dark brown, and placed forward on the head.
***Ears*—**The ears are small, triangular, placed high on the head, and, when at attention, very erect. A drop ear or ears is a disqualification.
***Nose*—**The nose is small and black.
***Bite*—**The bite must be scissors or level. Any deviation is to be severely penalized.

Neck, Topline, Body—*Neck*—The neck is of moderate length, slightly arched and in balance with the rest of the dog to give the correct silhouette. **Topline**—The topline is level or sloping from the withers to the croup. The stand-out ruff adds to the slope, making the dog seem slightly higher at the shoulders than at the rump. **Body**—The chest is broad and deep, and reaches to the elbows. The well sprung ribs (modified oval) are wide behind the shoulders and taper to the sternum. The forechest extends in front of the shoulders between the front legs. The loin is short, muscular and moderately drawn up. The croup is broad and well rounded with the tail docked. No tail is visually discernible.

Forequarters—The shoulders are well laid back, with the legs extending straight down from the body when viewed from the front. From the side, legs are placed well under the body. Pasterns are short, thick and strong, but still flexible, showing a slight angle when viewed from the side. Dewclaws are generally removed. Feet are small, round and tight. Nails are short, strong and black.

Hindquarters—The hindquarters appear slightly lighter than the fore-quarters, but are well muscled, and in balance with the front. The hocks are well let down and the stifles are well bent. Extreme angulation is to be penalized. From the rear, the legs extend straight down from the hip through the hock to the feet. Dew-claws must be removed.

Coat—**Pattern**—The adult coat is highly characteristic and must include several distinct lengths growing naturally in a specific pattern. The coat is short on the face, ears, front of the forelegs and on the hocks; it is medium length on the body, and longer in the ruff, cape, jabot and culottes. The ruff begins in back of the ears and extends completely around

The Schipperke's expression is mischievous and alert.

the neck; the cape forms an additional distinct layer extending beyond the ruff; the jabot extends across the chest and down between the front legs. The hair down the middle of the back, start-ing just behind the cape and continu-ing over the rump, lies flat. It is slightly shorter than the cape but longer than the hair on the sides of the body and sides of the legs. The coat on the rear of the thighs forms culottes, which should be as long as the ruff. Lack of differentiation in coat lengths should be heavily penalized, as it is an essen-tial breed characteristic.

Texture—The coat is abundant, straight and slightly harsh to the touch. The softer undercoat is dense and short on the body and is very dense around the neck, making the ruff stand out. Silky coats, body coats over three inches in length or very short harsh coats are equally incorrect.

Trimming—As the Schipperke is a natural breed only trimming of the whiskers and the hair between the pads of the feet is optional. Any other trimming must not be done.

Color—The outercoat must be black. Any color other than a natural black is a disqualification. The undercoat, however, may be slightly lighter. During the shedding period, the coat might take on a transitory reddish cast, which is to be penalized to the degree that it detracts from the overall black appearance of the dog. Graying due to age (seven years or older) or occasional white hairs should not be penalized.

Gait—Proper Schipperke movement is a smooth, well coordinated and graceful trot (basically double tracking at a moderate speed), with a tendency to gradually converge toward the center of balance beneath the dog as speed increases. Front and rear must be in perfect balance with good reach in front and drive in the rear. The topline remains level or slightly sloping downward from the shoulders to the rump. Viewed from the front, the elbows remain close to the body. The legs form a straight line from the shoulders through the elbows to the toes, with the feet pointing straight ahead. From the rear, the legs form a straight line from the hip through the hocks to the pads, with the feet pointing straight ahead.

Temperament—The Schipperke is curious, interested in everything around him, and is an excellent and faithful little watchdog. He is reserved with strangers and ready to protect his family and property if necessary. He displays a confident and independent personality, reflecting the breed's original purpose as watchdog and hunter of vermin.

DISQUALIFICATIONS
A drop ear or ears.
Any color other than a natural black.

Approved November 13, 1990
Effective January 1, 1991
Reprinted with permission of:
The Schipperke Club of America, Inc.

Index

If you are thinking of getting a Schipperke, this book will help you get acquainted with the breed. It will show you how to care for your Schipperke from puppyhood to adult, how to train it, and how to feed it. But, more important, it will help you understand the unique personality of this breed. Schipperkes may look cuddly and cute, but they have an exceptionally high level of energy and an independent nature that makes them far from the ideal dog for many people. Their small size can fool you, but these *are* big dogs in small bodies. They are highly intelligent and easily bored if not challenged with plenty of activity and exercise. They are great companions and devoted household guardians, but people with small children or yards without fences ought to look for another breed. This book tells you why.